C000295606

HOW TO **BUILD** A **PATINA** VOLKSWAGEN

Including Bugs, Buses and Derivatives

Mark Walker

1½-litre GP Racing 1961-1965 (Whitelock)
AC Two-litre Saloons & Buckland Sportscars (Archibald)
Alfa Romeo 155/156/147 Competition Touring Cars (Collins)
Alfa Romeo Giulia Coupé GT & GTA (Tipler)
Alfa Romeo Montreal – The dream car that came true (Taylor)
Alfa Romeo Montreal – The Essential Companion (Classic Reprint of 500 copies) (Taylor)
Alfa Tipo 33 (McDonough & Collins)
Alpine & Renault – The Development of the Revolutionary Turbo F1 Car 1968 to 1979 (Smith)
Alpine & Renault – The Sports Prototypes 1963 to 1969 (Smith)
Alpine & Renault – The Sports Prototypes 1973 to 1978 (Smith)
An Austin Anthology (Stringer)
An Austin Anthology II (Stringer)
An English Car Designer Abroad (Birtwhistle)
An Incredible Journey (Falls & Reisch)
Anatomy of the Classic Mini (Huthert & Ely)
Anatomy of the Works Minis (Moylan)
Armstrong-Siddeley (Smith)
Art Deco and British Car Design (Down)
Austin Cars 1948 to 1990 – A Pictorial History (Rowe)
Autodrome (Collins & Ireland)
Automotive A-Z, Lane's Dictionary of Automotive Terms (Lane)
Automotive Mascots (Kay & Springate)
Bahamas Speed Weeks, The (O'Neil)
Bentley Continental, Corniche and Azure (Bennett)
Bentley MkVI, Rolls-Royce Silver Wraith, Dawn & Cloud/Bentley R & S-Series (Nutland)
Bluebird CN7 (Stevens)
BMC Competitions Department Secrets (Turner, Chambers & Browning)
BMW 5-Series (Cranswick)
BMW Z-Cars (Taylor)
BMW Boxer Twins 1970-1995 Bible, The (Falloon)
BMW Cafe Racers (Cloesen)
BMW Classic 5 Series 1972 to 2003 (Cranswick)
BMW Custom Motorcycles – Choppers, Cruisers, Bobbers, Trikes & Quads (Cloesen)
Bonjour – Is this Italy? (Turner)
British 250cc Racing Motorcycles (Pereira)
British at Indianapolis, The (Wagstaff)
British Café Racers (Cloesen)
British Cars, The Complete Catalogue of, 1895-1975 (Culshaw & Horrobin)
British Custom Motorcycles – The Brit Chop – choppers, cruisers, bobbers & trikes (Cloesen)
BRM – A Mechanic's Tale (Salmon)
BRM V16 (Ludvigsen)
BSA Bantam Bible, The (Henshaw)
BSA Motorcycles – the final evolution (Jones)
Bugatti – The eight-cylinder Touring Cars 1920-34 (Price & Arbey)
Bugatti Type 40 (Price)
Bugatti 46/50 Updated Edition (Price & Arbey)
Bugatti T44 & T49 (Price & Arbey)
Bugatti 57 2nd Edition (Price)
Bugatti Type 57 Grand Prix – A Celebration (Tomlinson)
Caravan, Improve & Modify Your (Porter)
Caravans, The Illustrated History 1919-1959 (Jenkinson)
Caravans, The Illustrated History From 1960 (Jenkinson)
Carrera Panamericana, La (Tipler)
Car-tastrophes – 80 automotive atrocities from the past 20 years (Honest John, Fowler)
Chevrolet Corvette (Starkey)
Chrysler 300 – America's Most Powerful Car 2nd Edition (Ackerson)
Chrysler PT Cruiser (Ackerson)
Citroën DS (Bobbitt)
Classic British Car Electrical Systems (Astley)
Cobra – The Real Thing! (Legate)
Cobra, The last Shelby – My times with Carroll Shelby (Theodore)
Competition Car Aerodynamics 3rd Edition (McBeath)
Competition Car Composites A Practical Handbook (Revised 2nd Edition) (McBeath)
Concept Cars, How to illustrate and design – New 2nd Edition (Dewey)
Cortina – Ford's Bestseller (Robson)
Cosworth – The Search for Power (6th edition) (Robson)
Coventry Climax Racing Engines (Hammill)
Cranswick on Porsche (Cranswick)
Daily Mirror 1970 World Cup Rally 40, The (Robson)
Daimler SP250 New Edition (Long)
Datsun Fairlady Roadster to 280ZX – The Z-Car Story (Long)
Dino – The V6 Ferrari (Long)
Dodge Challenger & Plymouth Barracuda (Grist)
Dodge Charger – Enduring Thunder (Ackerson)
Dodge Dynamite! (Grist)
Dodge Viper (Zatz)
Dorset from the Sea – The Jurassic Coast from Lyme Regis to Old Harry Rocks photographed from its best viewpoint (also Souvenir Edition) (Belasco)
Draw & Paint Cars – How to (Gardiner)
Drive on the Wild Side, A – 20 Extreme Driving Adventures From Around the World (Weaver)
Driven – An Elegy to Cars, Roads & Motorsport (Aston)
Ducati 750 Bible, The (Falloon)
Ducati 750 SS 'round-case' 1974, The Book of the (Falloon)
Ducati 860, 900 and Mille Bible, The (Falloon)
Ducati Monster Bible (New Updated & Revised Edition), The (Falloon)
Ducati Story, The – 6th Edition (Falloon)
Ducati 916 (updated edition) (Falloon)
Dune Buggy, Building A – The Essential Manual (Shakespeare)
Dune Buggy Files (Hale)
Dune Buggy Handbook (Hale)
East German Motor Vehicles in Pictures (Suhr/Weinreich)
Essential Guide to Driving in Europe, The (Parish)
Fast Ladies – Female Racing Drivers 1888 to 1970 (Bouzanquet)
Fate of the Sleeping Beauties, The (op de Weegh/Hottendorff/op de Weegh)
Ferrari 288 GTO, The Book of the (Sackey)
Ferrari 333 SP (O'Neil)
Fiat & Abarth 124 Spider & Coupé (Tipler)
Fiat & Abarth 500 & 600 – 2nd Edition (Bobbitt)
Fiats, Great Small (Ward)
Fine Art of the Motorcycle Engine, The (Peirce)
Ford Cleveland 335-Series V8 engine 1970 to 1982 – The Essential Source Book (Hammill)
Ford F100/F150 Pick-up 1948-1996 (Ackerson)
Ford F150 Pick-up 1997-2005 (Ackerson)
Ford Focus WRC (Robson)
Ford GT – Then, and Now (Streather)
Ford GT40 (Legate)
Ford Midsize Muscle – Fairlane, Torino & Ranchero (Cranswick)
Ford Model Y (Roberts)
Ford Mustang II & Pinto 1970 to 80 (Cranswick)
Ford Small Block V8 Racing Engines 1962-1970 – The Essential Source Book (Hammill)
Ford Thunderbird From 1954, The Book of the (Long)
Ford versus Ferrari – The battle for supremacy at Le Mans 1966 (Starkey)
Formula 1 - The Knowledge 2nd Edition (Hayhoe)
Formula 1 All The Races - The First 1000 (Smith)
Formula One – The Real Score? (Harvey)
Formula 5000 Motor Racing, Back then ... and back now (Lawson)
Forza Minardi! (Vigar)
France: the essential guide for car enthusiasts – 200 things for the car enthusiast to see and do (Parish)
Franklin's Indians (Sucher/Pickering/Diamond/Havelin)
From Crystal Palace to Red Square – A Hapless Biker's Road to Russia (Turner)
Funky Mopeds (Skelton)
The Good, the Mad and the Ugly ... not to mention Jeremy Clarkson (Dron)
Grand Prix Ferrari – The Years of Enzo Ferrari's Power, 1948-1980 (Pritchard)
Grand Prix Ford – DFV-powered Formula 1 Cars (Robson)
GT – The World's Best GT Cars 1953-73 (Dawson)
Hillclimbing & Sprinting – The Essential Manual (Short & Wilkinson)
Honda NSX (Long)
Immortal Austin Seven (Morgan)
India - The Shimmering Dream (Reisch/Falls (translator))
Inside the Rolls-Royce & Bentley Styling Department – 1971 to 2001 (Hull)
Intermeccanica – The Story of the Prancing Bull (McCredie & Reisner)
Italian Cafe Racers (Cloesen)
Italian Custom Motorcycles (Cloesen)
Jaguar - All the Cars (4th Edition) (Thorley)
Jaguar from the shop floor (Martin)
Jaguar E-type Factory and Private Competition Cars (Griffiths)
Jaguar, The Rise of (Price)
Jaguar XJ 220 – The Inside Story (Moreton)
Jaguar XJ-S, The Book of the (Long)
Japanese Custom Motorcycles – The Nippon Chop – Chopper, Cruiser, Bobber, Trikes and Quads (Cloesen)
Jeep CJ (Ackerson)
Jeep Wrangler (Ackerson)
The Jowett Jupiter – The car that leaped to fame (Nankivell)
Karmann-Ghia Coupé & Convertible (Bobbitt)
Kawasaki Triples Bible, The (Walker)
Kawasaki W, H1 & Z – The Big Air-cooled Machines (Long)
Kawasaki Z1 Story, The (Sheehan)
Kris Meeke – Intercontinental Rally Challenge Champion (McBride)
KTM X-Bow (Pathmanathan)
Lamborghini Miura Bible, The (Sackey)
Lamborghini Murciélago, The book of the (Pathmanathan)
Lamborghini Urraco, The Book of the (Landsem)
Lambretta Bible, The (Davies)
Lancia 037 (Collins)
Lancia Delta HF Integrale (Blaettel & Wagner)
Lancia Delta Integrale (Collins)
Land Rover Design - 70 years of success (Hull)
Land Rover Emergency Vehicles (Taylor)
Land Rover Series III Reborn (Porter)
Land Rover, The Half-ton Military (Cook)
Land Rovers in British Military Service – coil sprung models 1970 to 2007 (Taylor)
Laverda Twins & Triples Bible 1968-1986 (Falloon)
Lea-Francis Story, The (Price)
Le Mans Panoramic (Ireland)
Lexus Story, The (Long)
Little book of microcars, the (Quellin)
Little book of smart, the – New Edition (Jackson)
Little book of trikes, the (Quellin)
Lola – The Illustrated History (1957-1977) (Starkey)
Lola – All the Sports Racing & Single-seater Racing Cars 1978-1997 (Starkey)
Lola T70 – The Racing History & Individual Chassis Record – 4th Edition (Starkey)
Lotus 18 Colin Chapman's U-turn (Whitelock)
Lotus 49 (Oliver)
Lotus Elan and Plus 2 Source Book (Vale)
Making a Morgan (Hensing)
Marketingmobiles, The Wonderful Wacky World of (Hale)
Maserati 250F In Focus (Pritchard)
Mazda MX-5/Miata 1.6 Enthusiast's Workshop Manual (Grainger & Shoemark)
Mazda MX-5/Miata 1.8 Enthusiast's Workshop Manual (Grainger & Shoemark)
Mazda MX-5 Miata, The book of the – The 'Mk1' NA-series 1988 to 1997 (Long)
Mazda MX-5 Miata, The book of the – The 'Mk2' NB-series 1997 to 2004 (Long)
Mazda MX-5 Miata Roadster (Long)
Mazda Rotary-engined Cars (Cranswick)
Maximum Mini (Booij)
Meet the English (Bowie)
Mercedes-Benz SL – R230 series 2001 to 2011 (Long)
Mercedes-Benz SL – W113-series 1963-1971 (Long)
Mercedes-Benz SL & SLC – 107-series 1971-1989 (Long)
Mercedes-Benz SLK – R170 series 1996-2004 (Long)
Mercedes-Benz SLK – R171 series 2004-2011 (Long)
Mercedes-Benz W123-series – All models 1976 to 1986 (Long)
Mercedes G-Wagen (Long)
MG, Made in Abingdon (Frampton)
MGA (Price Williams)
MGB & MGB GT– Expert Guide (Auto-doc Series) (Williams)
MGB Electrical Systems Updated & Revised Edition (Astley)
MGB – The Illustrated History, Updated Fourth Edition (Wood & Burrell)
The MGC GTS Lightweights (Morys)
Micro Caravans (Jenkinson)
Micro Trucks (Mort)
Microcars at Large! (Quellin)
Mike the Bike – Again (Macauley)
Mini Cooper – The Real Thing! (Tipler)
Mini Minor to Asia Minor (West)
Mitsubishi Lancer Evo, The Road Car & WRC Story (Long)
Montlhéry, The Story of the Paris Autodrome (Boddy)
MOPAR Muscle – Barracuda, Dart & Valiant 1960-1980 (Cranswick)
Morgan Maverick (Lawrence)
Morgan 3 Wheeler – back to the future!, The (Dron)
Morris Minor, 70 Years on the Road (Newell)
Moto Guzzi Sport & Le Mans Bible, The (Falloon)
Moto Guzzi Story, The – 3rd Edition (Falloon)
Motor Movies – The Posters! (Veysey)
Motor Racing – Reflections of a Lost Era (Carter)
Motor Racing – The Pursuit of Victory 1930-1962 (Carter)
Motor Racing – The Pursuit of Victory 1963-1972 (Wyatt/Sears)
Motor Racing Heroes – The Stories of 100 Greats (Newman)
Motorcycle Apprentice (Cakebread)
Motorcycle GP Racing in the 1960s (Pereira)
Motorcycle Racing with the Continental Circus 1920-1970 (Pereira)
Motorcycle Road & Racing Chassis Designs (Noakes)
Motorcycles and Motorcycling in the USSR from 1939 (Turbett)
Motorcycling in the '50s (Clew)
Motorhomes, The Illustrated History (Jenkinson)
Motorsport In colour, 1950s (Wainwright)
MV Agusta Fours, The book of the classic (Falloon)
N.A.R.T. – A concise history of the North American Racing Team 1957 to 1983 (O'Neil)
Nissan 300ZX & 350Z – The Z-Car Story (Long)
Nissan GT-R Supercar: Born to race (Gorodji)
Nissan – The GTP & Group C Racecars 1984-1993 (Starkey)
Northeast American Sports Car Races 1950-1959 (O'Neil)
Norton Commando Bible – All models 1968 to 1978 (Henshaw)
Nothing Runs – Misadventures in the Classic, Collectable & Exotic Car Biz (Slutsky)
Off-Road Giants! (Volume 1) – Heroes of 1960s Motorcycle Sport (Westlake)
Off-Road Giants! (Volume 2) – Heroes of 1960s Motorcycle Sport (Westlake)
Off-Road Giants! (Volume 3) – Heroes of 1960s Motorcycle Sport (Westlake)
Patina Volkswagens (Walker)
Pass the Theory and Practical Driving Tests (Gibson & Hoole)
Peking to Paris 2007 (Young)
Pontiac Firebird – New 3rd Edition (Cranswick)
Porsche 356 (2nd Edition) (Long)
Porsche 356, The Ultimate Book of the (Long)
Porsche 908 (Födisch, Neßhöver, Roßbach, Schwarz & Roßbach)
Porsche 911 Carrera – The Last of the Evolution (Corlett)
Porsche 911R, RS & RSR, 4th Edition (Starkey)
Porsche 911 SC, Clusker
Porsche 911, The Book of the (Long)
Porsche 911 – The Definitive History 1963-1971 (Long)
Porsche 911 – The Definitive History 1971-1977 (Long)
Porsche 911 – The Definitive History 1977-1987 (Long)
Porsche 911 – The Definitive History 1987-1997 (Long)
Porsche 911 – The Definitive History 1997-2004 (Long)
Porsche 911 – The Definitive History 2004-2012 (Long)
Porsche 911, The Ultimate Book of the Air-cooled (Long)
Porsche – The Racing 914s (Smith)
Porsche 911SC 'Super Carrera' – The Essential Companion (Streather)
Porsche 914 & 914-6: The Definitive History of the Road & Competition Cars (Long)
Porsche 924 (Long)
The Porsche 924 Carreras – evolution to excellence (Smith)
Porsche 928 (Long)
Porsche 930 to 935: The Turbo Porsches (Starkey)
Porsche 944 (Long)
Porsche 964, 993 & 996 Data Plate Code Breaker (Streather)
Porsche 993 'King Of Porsche' – The Essential Companion (Streather)
Porsche 996 'Supreme Porsche' – The Essential Companion (Streather)
Porsche 997 2004-2012 'Porsche Excellence' – The Essential Companion (Streather)
Porsche Boxster – The 986 series 1996-2004 (Long)
Porsche Boxster & Cayman – The 987 series (2004-2013) (Long)
Porsche Racing Cars – 1953 to 1975 (Long)
Porsche Racing Cars – 1976 to 2005 (Long)
Porsche - Silver Steeds (Smith)
Porsche – The Rally Story (Meredith)
Porsche: Three Generations of Genius (Meredith)
Powered by Porsche (Smith)
Preston Tucker & Others (Linde)
RAC Rally Action! (Gardiner)
Racing Classic Motorcycles (Reynolds)
Racing Colours – Motor Racing Compositions 1908-2009 (Newman)
Racing Line – British motorcycle racing in the golden age of the big single (Guntrip)
Racing Mustangs – An International Photographic History 1964-1986 (Holmes)
Rallye Sport Fords: The Inside Story (Moreton)
The Red Baron's Ultimate Ducati Desmo Manual (Cabrera Choclán)
Renewable Energy Home Handbook, The (Porter)
Roads with a View – England's greatest views and how to find them by road (Corfield)
Rolls-Royce Silver Shadow/Bentley T Series Corniche & Camargue – Revised & Enlarged Edition (Bobbitt)
Rolls-Royce Silver Spirit, Silver Spur & Bentley Mulsanne 2nd Edition (Bobbitt)
Rootes Cars of the 50s, 60s & 70s – Hillman, Humber, Singer, Sunbeam & Talbot, A Pictorial History (Rowe)
Rover Cars 1945 to 2005, A Pictorial History
Rover P4 (Bobbitt)
Runways & Racers (O'Neil)
Russian Motor Vehicles – Soviet Limousines 1930-2003 (Kelly)
Russian Motor Vehicles – The Czarist Period 1784 to 1917 (Kelly)
RX-7 – Mazda's Rotary Engine Sports car (Updated & Revised New Edition) (Long)
Sauber-Mercedes – The Group C Racecars 1985-1991 (Starkey)
Schlumpf – The intrigue behind the most beautiful car collection in the world (Op de Weegh & Op de Weegh)
Scooters & Microcars, The A-Z of Popular (Dan)
Scooter Lifestyle (Grainger)
Scooter Mania! – Recollections of the Isle of Man International Scooter Rally (Jackson)
Singer Story: Cars, Commercial Vehicles, Bicycles & Motorcycle (Atkinson)
Sleeping Beauties USA – abandoned classic cars & trucks (Marek)
SM – Citroën's Maserati-engined Supercar (Long & Claverol)
Speedway – Auto racing's ghost tracks (Collins & Ireland)
Sprite Caravans, The Story of (Jenkinson)
Standard Motor Company, The Book of the (Robson)
Steve Hole's Kit Car Cornucopia – Cars, Companies, Stories, Facts & Figures: the UK's kit car scene since 1949 (Hole)
Subaru Impreza: The Road Car And WRC Story (Long)
Supercar, How to Build your own (Thompson)
Suzuki Motorcycles - The Classic Two-stroke Era (Long)
Tales from the Toolbox (Oliver)
Tatra – The Legacy of Hans Ledwinka, Updated & Enlarged Collector's Edition of 1500 copies (Margolius & Henry)
Taxi! The Story of the 'London' Taxicab (Bobbitt)
This Day in Automotive History (Corey)
To Boldly Go – twenty six vehicle designs that dared to be different (Hull)
Toleman Story, The (Hilton)
Toyota Celica & Supra, The Book of Toyota's Sports Coupés (Long)
Toyota MR2 Coupés & Spyders (Long)
Triumph & Standard Cars 1945 to 1984 (Warrington)
Triumph Bonneville Bible (59-83) (Henshaw)
Triumph Bonneville!, Save the – The inside story of the Meriden Workers' Co-op (Rosamond)
Triumph Cars – The Complete Story (new 3rd edition) (Robson)
Triumph Motorcycles & the Meriden Factory (Hancox)
Triumph Speed Twin & Thunderbird Bible (Woolridge)
Triumph Tiger Cub Bible (Estall)
Triumph Trophy Bible (Woolridge)
Triumph TR6 (Kimberley)
TT Talking – The TT's most exciting era – As seen by Manx Radio TT's lead commentator 2004-2012 (Lambert)
Two Summers – The Mercedes-Benz W196R Racing Car (Ackerson)
TWR Story, The – Group A (Hughes & Scott)
TWR's Le Mans Winning Jaguars (Starkey)
Unraced (Collins)
Velocette Motorcycles – MSS to Thruxton – Third Edition (Burris)
Vespa – The Story of a Cult Classic in Pictures (Uhlig)
Vincent Motorcycles: The Untold Story since 1946 (Guyony & Parker)
Volkswagen Bus Book, The (Bobbitt)
Volkswagen Bus or Van to Camper, How to Convert (Porter)
Volkswagen Type 4, 411 and 412 (Cranswick)
Volkswagens of the World (Glen)
VW Beetle Cabriolet – The full story of the convertible Beetle (Bobbitt)
VW Beetle – The Car of the 20th Century (Copping)
VW Bus – 40 Years of Splitties, Bays & Wedges (Copping)
VW Bus Book, The (Bobbitt)
VW Golf: Five Generations of Fun (Copping & Cservenka)
VW – The Air-cooled Era (Copping)
VW T5 Camper Conversion Manual (Porter)
VW Campers (Copping)
Volkswagen Type 3, The book of the – Concept, Design, International Production Models & Development (Glen)
Volvo Estate, The (Hollebone)
You & Your Jaguar XK8/XKR – Buying, Enjoying, Maintaining, Modifying – New Edition (Thorley)
Which Oil? – Choosing the right oils & greases for your antique, vintage, veteran, classic or collector car (Michell)
Wolseley Cars 1948 to 1975 (Rowe)
Works MGs, The (Allison & Browning)
Works Minis, The Last (Purves & Brenchley)
Works Rally Mechanic (Moylan)

SpeedPro Series
4-Cylinder Engine Short Block High-Performance Manual – New Updated & Revised Edition (Hammill)
Aerodynamics of Your Road Car, Modifying the (Edgar and Barnard)
Camshafts – How to Choose & Time Them For Maximum Power (Hammill)
Custom Air Suspension – How to install air suspension in your road car – on a budget! (Edgar)
Cylinder Heads, How to Build, Modify & Power Tune – Updated & Revised Edition (Burgess & Gollan)
Distributor-type Ignition Systems, How to Build & Power Tune – New 3rd Edition (Hammill)
Fast Road Car, How to Plan and Build – Revised & Updated Colour New Edition (Stapleton)
Holley Carburetors, How to Build & Power Tune – Revised & Updated Edition (Hammill)
Mini Engines, How to Power Tune On a Small Budget – Colour Edition (Hammill)
Motorcycle-engined Racing Cars, How to Build (Pashley)
Motorsport, Getting Started in (Collins)
Nitrous Oxide High-performance Manual, The (Langfield)
Optimising Car Performance Modifications (Edgar)
Race & Trackday Driving Techniques (Hornsey)
Retro or classic car for high-performance, How to modify your (Stapleton)
Secrets of Speed – Today's techniques for four-stroke engine blueprinting & tuning (Swager)
Sports car & Kitcar Suspension & Brakes, How to Build & Modify – Revised 3rd Edition (Hammill)
SU Carburettor High-performance Manual (Hammill)
Successful Low-Cost Rally Car, How to Build a (Young)
V8 Engine, How to Build a Short Block For High-performance (Hammill)
Volkswagen Beetle Suspension, Brakes & Chassis, How to Modify For High-performance (Hale)
Volkswagen Bus Suspension, Brakes & Chassis for High-performance, How to Modify – Updated & Enlarged New Edition (Hale)
Weber DCOE, & Dellorto DHLA Carburetors, How to Build & Power Tune – 3rd Edition (Hammill)

Workshop Pro Series
Car Electrical and Electronic Systems (Edgar)
Modifying the Electronics of Modern Classic Cars (Edgar)
Setting up a Home Car Workshop (Edgar)

Enthusiast's Restoration Manual Series
Classic Car Bodywork, How to Restore (Thaddeus)
Classic Car Electrics (Thaddeus)
Classic Car Suspension, Steering & Wheels, How to Restore & Improve (Parish – translator)
Classic Cars, How to Paint (Thaddeus)
Ultimate Mini Restoration Manual, The (Ayre & Webber)
Volkswagen Beetle, How to Restore (Tyler)
VW Bay Window Bus (Paxton)
Yamaha FS1-E, How to Restore (Watts)

Essential Buyer's Guide Series
Volkswagen Bus (Copping)
Volkswagen Transporter T4 (1990-2003) (Copping/Cservenka)
VW Golf GTI (Copping)
VW Beetle (Copping)

www.veloce.co.uk Hubble & Hattie Kids Hubble & Hattie EARTHWORLD EXPANDING HORIZONS

First published in April 2020 by Veloce Publishing Limited, Veloce House, Parkway Farm Business Park, Middle Farm Way, Poundbury, Dorchester DT1 3AR, England.
Tel +44 (0)1305 260068 / Fax 01305 250479 / e-mail info@veloce.co.uk / web www.veloce.co.uk or www.velocebooks.com.
ISBN: 978-1-787115-00-2; UPC: 6-36847-01500-8.
© 2020 Mark Walker and Veloce Publishing. All rights reserved. With the exception of quoting brief passages for the purpose of review, no part of this publication may be recorded, reproduced or transmitted by any means, including photocopying, without the written permission of Veloce Publishing Ltd. Throughout this book logos, model names and designations, etc, have been used for the purposes of identification, illustration and decoration. Such names are the property of the trademark holder as this is not an official publication. Readers with ideas for automotive books, or books on other transport or related hobby subjects, are invited to write to the editorial director of Veloce Publishing at the above address. British Library Cataloguing in Publication Data – A catalogue record for this book is available from the British Library. Typesetting, design and page make-up all by Veloce Publishing Ltd on Apple Mac. Printed in India by Parksons Graphics.

HOW TO **BUILD** A **PATINA** VOLKSWAGEN

Including Bugs, Buses and Derivatives

Mark Walker

VELOCE PUBLISHING
THE PUBLISHER OF FINE AUTOMOTIVE BOOKS

Contents

Cover image: courtesy Andrew Thompson/AThompsonsPhoto. Endpapers: courtesy Austin Working and Stacey Wetnight

Introduction & acknowledgements

Over five years ago, when I began the journey of putting together the book proposal for *Patina Volkswagens*, I would never in my wildest dreams have figured that there would be more than one book; it was the publisher, or, more precisely, Rod Grainger at Veloce, who suggested a second book on Patination techniques. In actual fact, Rod suggested this in the same email where he agreed to publish *Patina Volkswagens*, but I decided to take some time to think about what kind of book this 'Techniques' book would be, and the book you see here is the result of that.

I've been pretty hands-on with building original paint and Patina Volkswagens over the past 15 years: first I ran 'The Bus Station,' where I got to build a lot of customer cars and personal builds, and later, after I decided to close The Bus Station for personal reasons, just building my own cars and writing 'How to' guides for *Volksworld* and *Volksworld Camper & Bus* magazines since 2012.

Many people wrongly assume that owning a Patina car is somehow lazy, but as you'll see contained within the pages of this book, Patina cars often take more creativity and, in some cases, are harder to pull off right than a fully restored car – the paint alone can take countless hours of trial and error, not to mention a lot of research to get right.

I'm sure it would be possible to put together a complete volume about paint and Patination techniques alone, but I'm sure it would take a lot of determination to read and digest – think *War and Peace*. With this in mind, and conscious that there's much more to building a Patina VW than the paint matching alone, I came up with *How to Build a Patina Volkswagen*.

It's a bit of a mouthful, but touches on a bit of everything you'll need to consider when thinking about building a car like this: what kind of Patina do you want? Stock suspension or raised/lowered suspension? What kind of products do you want to use to preserve the look? These, and lots of other questions, are things that have come up in conversation since I started the first book, and there wasn't enough room in *Patina Volkswagens* to cover even a fraction of it.

The great thing about this book is that there's room to showcase a lot of different Patina VWs that didn't

Standing in front of my original paint 1972 Single Cab Pickup at Volksworld Show 2019.
(Author's collection)

My most recent purchase: an original-paint 1966 Titian Red and Beige Grey Split Screen Bus. It's been off the road for 40 years, but will be back on the road in 2020. (Author's collection)

make it into *Patina Volkswagens*, which have been used to explain the many different ways in which you can build a Patina car and how, to some extent, the car that you choose to buy in the beginning will dictate the look of the finished product. Sure, you can add a lot of paint to a hardcore Patina car to make it look like a polished Patina car, but if there's a better candidate out there, why would you? If this book can help to guide you to the style of car you want to end up with before you buy, then that alone means that it's done its job.

Since the launch of *Patina Volkswagens*, I've been blown away with all of the comments and compliments about the book. If I'm brutally honest, I wrote the book that I'd always wanted to write – it was a passion project about a subject close to my heart, and I'm really happy that there are a lot of kindred spirits out there, for whom Patina has become an addiction and a way of life. If you're reading this and haven't yet seen or read *Patina Volkswagens*, then pick up a copy – it's not just a coffee table picture book, it covers the history of the Patina car and Patina VW scene.

I hope you enjoy this volume and that it offers guidance, helping you to tackle areas of car restoration and repair that you'd never thought of personally attempting. I knew I wanted to weld and restore cars back in 2002, but didn't have the skills; TV shows, certain people I knew, and countless other guys building VWs on internet forums inspired me to learn and try things myself, and I've found it a great creative

outlet. There's no greater satisfaction than being able to buy a project car knowing that you can fix it yourself, and even greater satisfaction comes when you look at a finished car and say to yourself: "I did that."

Most of the Patina VWs you would have seen on the internet or at any car show ten years ago would have been lowered. Go to a VW show today and you'll see a mixture of Patina VWs that are stock height, some that have been lowered, or even some that have raised suspension. I've built several stock height and lowered cars over the last few years, and I'm currently planning to build a raised one – a Patina Baja Bug. Some people are firmly rooted in one camp, but I like to think variety is the spice of life, and I always have a fairly long 'bucket list' of car builds. I've also built enough cars now that, whenever I see a picture of a potential project, I know exactly how I would build it, down to the wheels, suspension, and fine details. It's an illness, but one I'm happy to have.

Acknowledgements

In putting a book like this together, there are literally hundreds of people I could thank. Those who inspired me by writing their own VW books that formulated a large part of my childhood, and those that built cars that drew me into the world of modified cars and classic VWs in the first place. I'd also like to thank everyone who helped in any way with both of the Patina Volkswagens books, especially with pictures and information.

Thanks must also go to the guys at Curve Media, who gave me the opportunity to work on a Patina car as I put this book together – the car will be featured on a forthcoming episode of the *Salvage Hunters: Classic Cars* TV show on Discovery Network. Big thanks also to Jason Baldwin of Hampshire-based Dub Works, for giving me the space to work on the car, and to Steve Parsons for help with sympathetically adding Patina, and allowing me to use pictures of this in the book.

I'd like to thank my parents, for supporting my hobby over the years – mum for driving me to the local drag strip and VW shows before I could even drive. Most of all, though, I'd like to thank my better half Joanna (Jojo) Cooke; not only did she help me through the entire process, handle my PR through her company – Departure PR – and support me in times of need, but she also listens to me talking about cars on a daily basis.

CHAPTER ONE
Deciding on a look

To some, it may appear backwards to decide on how you want a finished Patina car to look first, even before you've searched for or bought a project vehicle. For many people who are into Patina cars, this thought may never have crossed their minds – I've lost count of how many times I've seen a Patina VW project car on the internet, for example, and completely lost my mind over it; even if that car isn't what I'm currently looking for, or the Patina is too hardcore for the damp, salty UK climate (especially where I live, near the beach). There are occasions where you see a car and just HAVE to own it. If you're armed with knowledge before you make a purchase though, then you're more likely to have a successful outcome, and more likely to keep the car when completed, rather than putting it up for sale.

As with any type and style of car, a 'Patina Volkswagen' means different things to different people. When people began to bring unrestored cars to shows, many of them were more 'Rat Look' than Patina as we know it now. Even now though, no two Patina car builds are ever the same, and this is what makes Patina cars so interesting. In this chapter, we'll explore all the different styles, from hardcore rat, all the way through to polished Patina and even different ways of faking Patina – 'fauxtina' – and we'll look at some of the methods people use when building Patina cars.

The reason that this chapter is the first chapter in a 'How to Build' book, is that it's usually the car that dictates the finished look: you're not making your life easy if you want to end up with a polished Patina car, but buy a rusted and dented car that is really only a suitable basis for a Rat Look or hardcore Patina car. Sure, you could spend countless hours repairing rust and damage, and paint blend and Patinate ¾ of the car to end up with your goal of a polished Patina car, but why would you if a little patience (or saving a little more money) might net a more worthy car?

Gareth Bayliss-Smith's early Squareback has enough Patina to get most Patina lovers salivating; this car is being subjected to a full body-off preservation build. Being that Type 3 repair panels aren't as widely available as Type 1 or 2 panels, Gareth is having to source some rust-free body cuts to carry out the metal restoration. (Courtesy Gareth Bayliss-Smith)

Controversial maybe, but why would you do all of this to a car when there are other cars out there that align better to your desired outcome?

These days, of course, demand is often greater than supply, at least when it comes to earlier cars. This means that people are more likely to carry out a greater amount of work on an early car, because it's hard or even impossible to find some of the rare models in great 'survivor' shape. Even so, some would say that turning a hardcore Patina car into a polished Patina car is no different than giving the same car a full restoration; they would argue that it's hardly going to be a truly original paint car or have original and genuine Patina when you're done with it.

All this being said, as Patina VWs have become increasingly popular, the supply of genuine rust and accident-free original paint cars has begun to dry up, or the prices have increased to the point they are out of reach for many. Practically everyone who is part of the Patina scene and regularly builds new project cars has had to adjust their expectations and start to buy some of the cars that haven't been so lucky when it comes to rust or accident damage – if you want to build a Patina car now and don't have a huge budget, this is the compromise.

When it comes to my own projects, I've seen a pattern over the last 15 years: where once I wouldn't buy a rare or early Split Screen Bus that needed even small rust repairs or had cut rear wheel wells, I now take on Split Screen and Bay Window Buses, and even late-model Bugs, that need a whole lot more work. It's a definite case of supply and demand, which has not only pushed up prices, but also made cars in much worse condition become desirable. I can assure you that if you had taken a trip around a VW junkyard five, ten, or 15 years ago and deemed everything as total junk, another walk around the same yard now would make you reconsider.

This has brought more late-model cars onto the scene, especially in the USA, where any model of VW younger than 1968 was once considered a 'Fat Chick' and disposable. What's more, people are generally more willing to take on serious rust repair and accident damage, whilst preserving and blending in the paint to match the original Patina. Whilst some still believe this is faking it, others, including myself, think that it's completely acceptable. Sympathetically matching the original paint on repaired areas is a far cry from building a fauxtina car – where the car is completely repainted then sanded down to resemble wear or original Patina – but even building a fauxtina car can be okay too, if it's done right. If you own a car, it's up to you to do with it as you please; this book aims to point you in the right direction.

Look at the pictures on this page (and the next) of a Montana Red 1969 Deluxe Bus. This is a Bus Craig Yelley built a couple of years ago – he stuck with saving the majority of the original paint against all the odds, even when the Bus needed a whole new front nose panel. Note the use of soft masking lines when blending the paint into the rear wheelarch panel – just one of the many tricks to blending new paint into old. (Courtesy Craig Yelley)

Putting the faux in fauxtina – when it's acceptable

The reason most people baulk at fauxtina, is that they are confusing properly replicated Patina with the 'fake rat' – sanding down all over in ways that the sun could never have burned the paint off, then leaving a car to rust, effectively destroying it, or at least shortening its lifespan. It's actually really difficult to match or create Patina on a car and make it look like original paint, much more difficult than simply repainting the whole car in many instances.

I'm sure a good few people are reading the above information about fauxtina and are maybe taking exception to it. Some people can't, no matter how hard they try, identify with what would make someone add fake Patina to a car. Later in the book we'll talk about stripping repainted layers off to get back to original paint. As you'll see, some cars respond to being stripped better than others: some types of paint are so resistant to being stripped, that the end product is just too far gone for some.

At what point do you draw a line under original paint? It's a rhetorical question and one that will have 1000 different answers depending on who you ask. For me personally, if the 'new' paint is so hard to get off, that it ends up leaving a lot of damage in the original paint, or the repaint layers are stripped to reveal original paint that has been attacked with 60 grit on a DA sander, which has removed a fair degree of the original paint and maybe some of the primer, then it's time for new paint. Controversial maybe, but that's my opinion.

However, I have no desire to own a restored or shiny-painted car for a variety of different reasons, and I know a lot of like-minded people with the same view. If you have a copy of *Patina Volkswagens*, you'll be familiar with the work of Craig Yelley. Craig runs 'Vintage VW' in Spokane, Washington, and he goes to great lengths on his Patina builds to preserve the original paint at all costs. Some people probably think Craig is crazy for doing what he does, and I know for a fact that 99 per cent of mainstream body shops just wouldn't get it either.

I know that a large percentage of people reading this book would get what Craig does and many would look at the red Bus on the previous page, and think it was original paint. That's as a result of Craig's skill and passion, though; he's passionate about original paint, and has taken the time to hone his skills when it comes to Patina paint blending and really studying Patina – figuring out how the model of VW he's currently working on would have faded naturally with the sun and working hard to replicate this. Most importantly, Craig never overdoes it with the Patina fade, he errs on the side of caution and stops when it looks natural.

I'm sure many of us are of the opinion that modern 2k paint is too shiny for these old vehicles – it looks like plastic and doesn't really suit 50-year-old cars. It also doesn't last like original paint and doesn't have any character. The other thing about shiny-paint cars is that they take a hell of a lot of bodywork and Bondo to get the arrow-straight finish you see on a restored car. For many of us, this eclipses all the character – the factory paint blemishes and runs, the visible factory spot welds, etc. Many people are also too scared to drive a restored car daily, or leave it in a supermarket car park, for instance. So, considering the above, what

This Indian Red 1960 looked like a fairly good car in the vendor's pictures, but needed extensive rust repair – the heater channels on both sides were replaced – and some accident repair too. (Author's collection)

Mid-way through an accident repair on my Indian Red 1960 Beetle. The paint was sympathetically blended in to match the surrounding Patina.
(Author's collection)

are your options when the original paint is so far gone that it can't be saved?

Patina style repaints don't contain the endless bodywork and filler work that a restoration-quality paint job requires – in the Patina world, we embrace original dings and dents to a large degree. Sure, we may choose to repair larger body damage on occasion or weld up rust holes and hacks, but we're not too precious about getting everything perfect, because, for us at least, imperfection **is** perfection.

Hopefully, you can see what I'm getting at – that many people will never do restored cars – and that it is, therefore, acceptable to either fauxtina parts of a car, or even a full car if the original paint can't be saved. Accepting that this kind of paintwork is usually necessary, even in some small degree, when building a Patina car, is the first step to realising that no car 'needs' to be fully restored – any car can have some degree of the character saved, even if it's only small amounts of the interior and exterior paint.

So, with that part behind us, let's look at the different Patina looks you can achieve with any car – it's simply a matter of locating a suitable car and working out which look you want to achieve, or being open to building a car in the style that the car you buy lends itself to.

Dave Ball's Squareback will need a fair amount of Patina paint blending in order for the new panels and repaired areas to match the existing paintwork. Does this mean that he should repaint the whole car though? This is a good example of when some good fauxtina paint blends can be worthwhile.
(Courtesy Dave Ball)

Hardcore Patina

Hardcore Patina cars are usually the most controversial; if you're outside of the car scene, you might look at a slammed Split Beetle like Gary Hilling's

car on this page and think it was a worthless pile of junk. You wouldn't see the countless thousands that have been invested in it, or the hundreds of hours working underneath it to make it drive well, as well as look right. You probably wouldn't even realise that it's probably worth more than double what many new cars would cost at the dealer.

Hardcore Patina cars have often had a hard life – not so hard that they have been in a huge accident, or got sent to the crusher, but usually hard enough that they've sustained either fairly significant body damage at some point, or major component failure. They've usually ended up in a junkyard, or parked in the searing heat and freezing winters for a few decades.

Gary Hilling's Split Beetle when it was first imported by Graham at FBI VW – making a car like this into a polished Patina car would be a lot of work.
(Courtesy Graham Clarke/FBI VW)

Gary and son Jake decided to leave the body on this car fairly rough, and just repair the worst of the rust and body damage – it still looks great.
(Courtesy Gary Hilling)

I bought this incredible hardcore Patina Oval Bug back in 2013, but decided to get a refund when it turned out to be on a much later floorpan. The car is now in France and back on the road.
(Author's collection)

Of course, Gary Hilling has done some work to the body of his Split Beetle to pound out some of the worst dents: the wings/fenders of this car were literally kicked in when it was discovered – but he chose not to try to get all of the panels arrow straight and paint blend everything all nice and shiny, to have done that would, to many, have been missing the point of this car somewhat. The way that Gary has built the car says "I've had a life, but I'm here against the odds – a true survivor in a world of throwaway objects."

Daniel Mandat bucked a trend – at least in the air-cooled VW scene – by using large diameter split rim wheels on his hardcore Patina build. (Courtesy Daniel Mandat)

Austin Working chose to seal and preserve the hardcore Patina on his incredible '68 Beetle by clearcoating the outside of the body. Car features a show quality body-off restoration with air ride suspension and a new interior.
(Courtesy Andrew Thompson/AThompsonsPhoto)

Survivor cars/barn find cars

Truly unspoiled survivor cars that need nothing or very little in terms of body repair or paintwork could be seen as the basis for a polished Patina car or given any number of different looks. I hate to say it, but some would even think a car like this is perfect for the Rat treatment. The difficulty with doing **anything** to a true survivor or barn find car, however, is that to do so will undoubtedly destroy its provenance. Anything beyond careful cleaning will serve to destroy the very reason that a car like this appeals to people in the first place. Like a fine antique or a house in the French

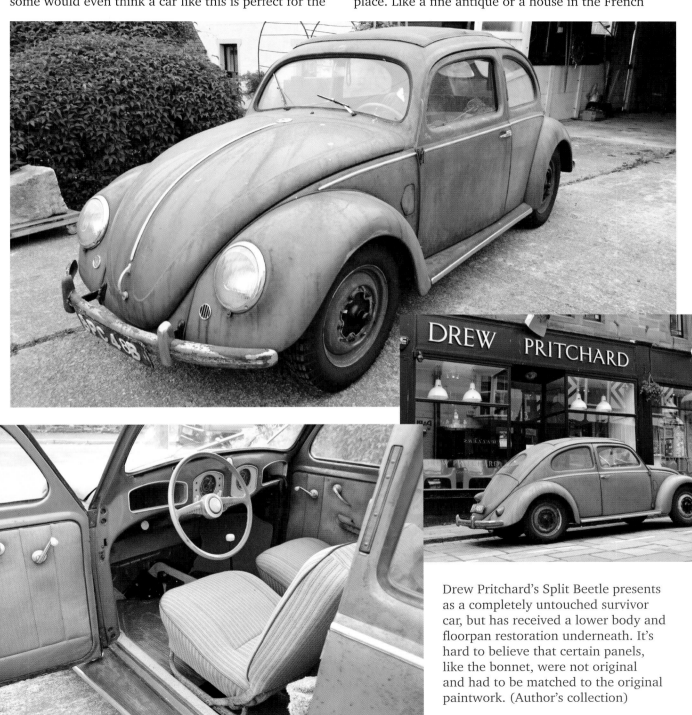

Drew Pritchard's Split Beetle presents as a completely untouched survivor car, but has received a lower body and floorpan restoration underneath. It's hard to believe that certain panels, like the bonnet, were not original and had to be matched to the original paintwork. (Author's collection)

PJ Gibbons' car is a true survivor – he did a preservation type restoration underneath and made some period correct modifications, but chose to leave the paint with a dulled finish. (Courtesy PJ Gibbons)

countryside with peeling paint on the shutters – the faded paint and time warp condition is the very reason that they are so attractive in their raw, as-found, state.

Case in point is Drew Pritchard's car – his '52 was featured in the *Patina Volkswagens* book, but actually cost over £20k from the original owner's estate as a project vehicle with missing parts and in need of rust repair. The sympathetic, preservation-style restoration of this car likely cost a fair few thousand more, and, even with the philosophy of minimum intervention that Drew has always held close to his heart, he wisely had the body taken off the pan and any rust repairs have been done right the first time. Although some would deride the fact that the floorpan has been restored and that the body is hardly untouched, the fact is that it's now a car that is safe to drive, has been freed of rust and preserved for future generations to enjoy. Perhaps most importantly, the work has been done so skilfully that it's pretty much impossible to tell that it has been done.

However, when I visited Drew to photograph the car, he mentioned that he regretted having the non-original bonnet matched (and it is a perfect match) to the existing Patina when it was sympathetically restored. He also has a tag on the original keys saying "Do not wash," in case a member of staff at his place of business mistakenly decided that the car needed cleaning. At the time, I didn't really get the 'do not wash' sentiment, but Drew knows antiques and has a mantra of minimum intervention – do the minimum amount that it takes to make something functional again.

Whilst I personally would still wash a car like this from time to time, I've learned from past mistakes, and certainly wouldn't be in a hurry to polish the paint on any of my future projects; I'd take some time to wash it first and figure out how far I should go. PJ Gibbons has done minimum intervention on the paintwork of his Split Beetle (pictured above) too and I totally get it – sure, he could have (and still could) polish the original paint to a mirror-like shine, but he understands that a large part of that car's appeal is faded and dull paintwork. To take away that aspect is to take away the raw appeal of that car in its entirety. I've said it before and I'll say it again: it's only original once. Sure, you could buff a car and then let it sit neglected until the paint fades, but it may never be the same as it was; paint takes years – decades, even – to mature to a fully dulled state.

Has PJ left the car entirely as he found it? No, he hasn't. There were several areas, especially on the wing/fender edges, where the rusted metal has been repaired, and the paint and Patina have been really carefully and sympathetically matched by Patina matching expert Steve Parsons. PJ could have had Steve go overboard and redo some of the old and mismatched paint repairs, but he didn't, he chose to leave those old repairs as a chapter in the car's life story, rather than over-restore the car and hide the poorly matched paint repairs away under new paint; minimum intervention.

Repainted Patina cars

Some would think that repainted cars – cars that are not original paint – would be a no-brainer when it comes to doing a Patina build. For many, the mantra is 'original paint at all costs.' For these people, there would never be any question about whether or not a

This Mouse Grey 1963 walkthru Bus was the largest project I have taken on to date. Having been sitting in a junkyard in Roswell, New Mexico since 1973, it had damage from a Beetle sitting on the roof, the 'usual' rust damage, and had also had large sections of the chassis cut out with a gas axe. (Author's collection)

My Mouse Grey '63 Bus after a mammoth seven-week effort to get it back on the road – the repairs were blended into the polished original paint. (Author's collection)

car should be stripped back to original paint. These are quite likely to also be the same people who would keep a car in original paint, even if 80 per cent of the original paint was lost or badly damaged. Others, though, are beginning to see that a car that was repainted in the 1970s will have worn that repaint for far longer than it ever sported original paint.

Whatever the colour or paint finish, there's no denying that a repaint can be a valid part of a car's life story. It may not satisfy the VW purists, who believe that every car should only wear the original paint colour that the VW factory painted it in. Ironically, many so-called purists prefer restored or repainted cars over original.

From a personal standpoint, I love original paint cars and wouldn't normally dream of repainting a car – if I ever did, I wouldn't be tempted to change the colour, but if a car has an old repaint that itself has nice Patina on it, I'd feel like it was a crime to strip this on the chance that I might find good original paint underneath.

Matt black or primer notwithstanding, I've seen a lot of repainted Patina VWs over the years that I would love to own and I wouldn't do a thing to them when it comes to the paint finish. I love original paint and I love original paint colours, but you have to admit, seeing a car that has been repainted in the 1970s, in a vastly different colour scheme than VW would have done, actually adds to some cars – it makes them stand out at car shows too, where most cars these days are painted in a Volkswagen shade.

Having seen a lot of these repainted survivor cars stripped back to original paint – in many cases losing great Patina, or even company logos that were applied over the repaint – I find it a bit of a shame that these repainted cars aren't really valued as survivors. People are so keen to discover if there's original paint underneath the repaint, that they often don't even give a minute's thought to cleaning what's there and working with it. As a result of this, repainted Patina cars are somewhat of a rarity, and definitely an endangered species.

continues page 21

When I stripped three different layers of paint off this Yukon Yellow 1962 Karmann Cabriolet for the *Salvage Hunters: Classic Cars* TV programme, no-one really knew what would be lurking underneath. While many would give up and repaint a car that was found to have several non-original panels, I chose to sympathetically blend the paint and match the Patina. (Author's collection)

Stacey Wetnight stripped the repaint from his '59 Euro Beetle and chose to leave the paint as is, with exposed scars and all. Many would have blended in some new paint, but the beauty of Patina cars is that they're very open to interpretation. (Courtesy Stacey Wetnight)

The unique Patina finish on Brett Elsmore's Karmann Ghia is a result of the car being painted brown over the original red paint. The brown paint then burned through, giving a unique finish. (Courtesy Brett Elsmore)

The Bob Saunders TV Bus is a good example of a repainted Bus with great Patina. People in the VW scene love original logos, and this Bus is a great example. (Author's collection)

Steve Sanchez' old Single Cab had been repainted back in the 1970s and logoed for 'Oud's Hardware Store.' Whilst not the original colour, the paint had an incredible time-worn Patina to it. A subsequent owner repainted the truck in the original Dove Blue. Steve took the truck back to visit the guy he bought it from and attempted to re-create the before picture. (Courtesy Steve Sanchez)

Mike Heywood's old Beetle had been repainted in a dark green over the original L380 Turkis paint. While many would have attempted to strip off the remains of the repaint, Mike chose to embrace the Patina, and gave the car a body-off preservation build. (Courtesy Joss Ashley)

Justin Heath's Notchback is a fine example of embracing the unique Patina bestowed upon a car by leaving the faded repaint layers, instead of stripping back to the original. Justin's car features a full show-quality build underneath. (Courtesy Melanie Perron)

This page and opposite: Discovered by Randy Carlsson in California, the original Auto Haus shop car from the 1970s was bought and shipped to France by Laurent 'El Dub' Dubois. The car was debuted at the 2019 European Bug-in after Laurent carried out a Patina preservation in secret. The car is a rare true survivor from the 'bad taste' '70s, complete with many rare period parts. (Author's collection)

Baja Bugs and '80s/'90s Cal Look

When it comes to the VW scene, Baja Bugs and '80s/'90s custom VWs are often looked down upon. They were popular in the 1970s and '80s/'90s, but they are now widely seen as 'hack jobs,' and people seem to get all hot under the collar about them. Why did someone 'ruin' an oval-window Bug by chopping off the front and rear bodywork, attaching a fibreglass kit and painting it with a 1970s colour scheme? For a long time, these cars have been like a bad smell under people's noses, and even when these cars did get 'saved,' it would be a case of welding on new front and rear bodywork and restoring to original.

Maybe this is controversial, but I've seen so many early '70s converted Baja Bugs and '80s Cal Look cars of late that, to me, just look right – they are of a period and are rare, gradually being eradicated by the restorers. Some would even go as far as calling these cars survivors – they tell a story of a time long past, a time when creativity was rewarded in the VW and worldwide car scenes. A time when the only limit to what you'd do to a car was your imagination. While many people frown upon these cars and view them as hacks, the same people may fit front tubs and chassis notches to a Bus they are lowering; this really isn't much different. What a lot of this comes down to is fashion and being afraid to go against the grain.

When you consider the above and how many junkyards clear out and crush cars every few years, the sheer fact that many of these early Bajas or '80s Cal Look cars have survived, against all those odds, really does make them survivor cars.

Build your car your way

This chapter is the first chapter for the above reasons and the pictures that illustrate this chapter are to help you, the reader, decide which cars and styles appeal to you the most. Maybe you're new to Patina cars, or perhaps you've been around the block a few times, have a few Patina car builds under your belt, and have a definite opinion about what appeals to you personally;

continues page 24

Discovered by Rusty Willey and put back on the road by Patrick Peet, this 1962 'Bug eye' Baja had a unique Patina paint scheme. Whilst not original paint, the Patina was incredible. The car was subsequently destroyed in an off-road accident. (Author's collection)

Austin Working bucked a trend in California by doing a full pan-off build on a 1968 Beetle. There's a lot of snobbery around late model cars, but no one can deny that this car has the look. (Courtesy Austin Working)

My old 1962 Single Cab was heavily modified and dropped to ride low. Modifications include chassis notches and a raised steering box. (Author's collection)

Some people were surprised when I built my '63 Mouse Grey Bus standard height; build the car you want, not to please others. (Author's collection)

Despite owning a stock height 1963 Bus at the same time, I decided that my '68 Sunroof Beetle needed to sit low on some Porsche Cosmic replica wheels. (Author's collection)

even if this is the case, it does help to re-evaluate from time to time and see if the same things float your boat that always did, or if you've gained a new appreciation for a different way of doing things.

Of course, it's not always the type of paint finish that might make you re-evaluate things. I used to run a company that was famed for lowering and suspension mods, and the first thing I would always do when I brought home a car would be to strip the suspension and drop whatever I'd bought closer to the ground, but my tastes have changed over time. Some of this may be due to 'getting old' and becoming tired of bottoming out on poor road surfaces and speed bumps. This is definitely the case when it comes to owning a camper, for instance, and wanting a relaxed drive when I'm in holiday mode.

Some of my change in taste comes down to liking many different types of air-cooled VWs, and by getting inspiration from other people's cars. Maybe it was one or two stock height Split Buses at car shows that really spoke to me, but, in 2013, I decided I wanted to buck a personal trend and build my '63 Mouse Grey Bus as a stock height camper, and I don't regret my decision.

In 2014, I decided to fit a 4in narrowed beam to my '68 Sunroof Beetle and lower it with Porsche pattern Cosmic wheels. It wasn't that I'd changed my mind again, but more a case that the '68 Beetle with heavy Patina did nothing for me as a standard height car, but did everything for me as a lowered one.

The original paint 1971 Bay Window Bus that I built in summer 2019 is one of those rare vehicles that would look great either lowered, stock height, or even with raised suspension and mud tyres – a look that is gaining in popularity right now. After months of going back and forth, I decided to polish the paint, leave the Bus standard height, and fit some slot mags for a look reminiscent of the early '70s. With the Sierra Yellow paint, it already looks very '70s, so the slot mags and some subtle vinyl stripes suit it.

The bottom line is this: take as much time as you need figuring out how you need to build your Patina VW, and ignore the opinions of others unless you ask for them. There are enough people in the scene who will give unsolicited advice and tell you what you should and shouldn't be doing with your car and your money. Maybe their hearts are in the right place and

Sometimes your vision for a car will fall flat when you finally see it done: I decided to build my 1971 Sierra Yellow Bus stock height with a set of slot mag wheels for a '70s vibe, but didn't like the finished look. (Author's collection)

Project cars like Al Speaight's Horizon Blue Canadian Standard Oval Beetle would be enough to tempt most hardcore Patina VW fans to find the money somehow. Although many would have gone down the hardcore Patina or Rat route with this car, Al chose to do some preservation restoration, and went down the stock height polished Patina route.
(Courtesy Al Speaight)

maybe they feel like they are stopping you from making a mistake, or 'ruining' a car, but it's your car and your money. Figure out what you want from the build and the finished product, then build it how you want to build it and enjoy it.

We each make many small decisions when we decide to take on a project and we draw inspiration from a wide variety of sources; inspiration is literally everywhere, so go with your hunch. As long as you feel passionate about how you build your car, and are mindful that you're just the owner of a car for a relatively short time, then you can't go far wrong. Ignore others and dance to the beat of your own drum – this is how crazes and styles come about, people innovate and others follow suit. Sure, some people won't like what you've done with your car, and may even bitch and moan about it, but it's your car and your right not to care what they think.

When it comes down to it, you can let the car you purchase dictate the finished look of your

While many choose to leave hardcore Patina cars in their raw and rust-stained 'as found' state, Tony Wysinger is one of the guys who pioneered the use of a product called 'CLR' to scrub off the rust staining, as he's done on this 1970 Bay Window junkyard find. As you can see, there's still a lot of the original primer left, having been hidden for decades under the rust staining.
(Courtesy Tony Wysinger)

project, or you can begin with a very distinct look in mind and be patient until a project car comes along that aligns with this. If you're unsure, or on the fence about how you'd like the finished car to look, then there's no substitute for looking at lots of different Patina VWs to give you project inspiration. Both this book and *Patina Volkswagens* should provide plenty of food for thought. This being said, your tastes may evolve over time, and, if your project takes a year or two, don't be surprised if you've changed your mind on style and wheel choices several times before it is finished. It happens to the best of us.

Before and after images of Gary Hilling's Split Beetle. It would have taken a lot of work to make this into a polished Patina car, but some would feel that it was a worthy candidate. Gary chose to pound out the worst of the dents, allowing the car to show off its life story. (Courtesy Gary Hilling)

"Most cars dictate the look of the finished build" – I had the vision of my original logoed Bay Window Pickup on large off-road tyres as soon as I clapped eyes on it. (Author's collection)

CHAPTER TWO

Buying a Patina project vehicle

Now that you've figured out exactly how you want your finished Patina build to look, we can get down to the nitty-gritty of sourcing the right vehicle. The aim of this chapter, is not only to point you in the right direction of where to look for Patina cars and Buses, but also to give you tips on inspecting a car yourself, distance buying – including having cars appraised, figuring out shipping and a description of each model when it comes to problem areas, rust damage, and poor repairs.

Finding cars locally

If you live in most parts of Europe – or any other cool/cold and damp climate, especially areas where they salt the roads in winter – then finding a Patina car locally that's in good enough shape to build into a Patina ride is probably quite unlikely. If you're based somewhere like certain parts of the USA, Northern Scandinavia, or, more specifically, an area where the climate is quite dry, then it's still possible that you could find a car right on your doorstep. Although it may seem completely crazy that, in this internet age where everyone seems to know the value of everything, there are still early Beetles and Buses being discovered with alarming regularity, and picked up for a few hundred, up to a few thousand, dollars.

Even if the owners of these cars – who likely parked them in a backyard because they stopped working,

Antoine Puygranier was lucky enough to find an early Turkis Ragtop Beetle practically on his doorstep; finding solid original paint cars in Europe is rare. (Courtesy Antoine Puygranier)

Kyle Golding created a social media buzz in 2018, finding this super-rare Binz Double Cab Pickup locally that had been sitting since the 1970s. Kyle is a serial VW hunter, and this was one of around 20 cars he saved in 2018 alone. (Courtesy Kyle Golding)

or sustained some accident damage – are on the internet, then it's likely that they can't be bothered with advertising the car, taking pictures, etc, or they may not need the money. Over the last 15 years, as prices of VW project cars on eBay USA, thesamba.com, Craigslist, and all other advertising platforms have crept up, many guys have taken to the back roads of their towns, cities, and more rural areas in search of old VWs just waiting for another shot on the road.

Social media, especially Instagram and Facebook, makes it possible for many of us to witness a few of these amazing discoveries. Worthy candidates for a Patina preservation type restoration are literally still being discovered every day, throughout the world; just last year, Kyle Golding – @goldingbuiltkyle on Instagram – found a super rare Binz Double Cab Pickup that had been sitting since the 1970s. He picked it up for a very reasonable price and has now put it back on the road where it belongs.

Kyle, like many other guys (and girls) buys a lot of old VWs mainly because they find him – if you drive around in an old Volkswagen, people often approach you to talk about the car you're driving and this often leads to: "I know where there's one like that" or "I have one in my backyard, you should come and check out." This is one tactic that a lot of the more prolific

Another of Kyle's discoveries, this '65 Beetle had been sitting in the second owner's garage since the 1990s – Kyle buffed the flat paint and lowered it with a 6in narrowed beam. (Courtesy Kyle Golding)

Serial VW hunter Steve Sanchez's '65 Beetle that was given a preservation type body-off restoration over the course of a few months in 2018/19. Steve now drives the back roads with this car hunting for old VWs. (Courtesy Steve Sanchez)

One of Steve's former daily drivers was this original paint '65 Double Cab – he put it back on the road with the help of his friend Craig Yelley back in 2008. (Courtesy Steve Sanchez)

car hunters know works to their advantage; some even go as far as putting stickers on their VWs saying 'I Buy Old Volkswagens' or similar.

Sure, you may be saying to yourself sarcastically, "sure, there are Split Buses and early Bugs everywhere, just ripe for picking". In a word, no, finding early model VWs in any condition sitting outside is getting much rarer. Shows like *American Pickers* have shown people the value in old VWs, and car shows where Split Buses are being sold at Barret Jackson auctions for over $200k have done nothing to help this either. Remember how I said in Chapter 1 about visiting the same junkyard again after five, ten, or 15 years and finding value in things you once dismissed? Well, this is exactly the same with cars on private properties.

To some – I like to say spoiled – people who live in dry areas, a 1966 Beetle or 1968 Bus would have been the kind of cars you dismissed out of hand five or ten years ago, especially if there were earlier cars or Buses on the same property. But how about if you visited the same place now, in a market where the '66 Bug and '68 Bus have become desirable by proxy or the laws of supply and demand? There are also the 'freak' purchases like Kyle's Binz. I was messaged by someone recently who'd unearthed a yard full of early cars in the Washington/Idaho area – there were at least two Patina Split Buses, and one had faded original logos!

Having watched VW forums and social media platforms over the last 20 years, I can think of a number of people for whom the scenario of going back for less desirable cars is playing out. Steve Sanchez from Spokane, Washington is just one guy who is a serial picker and collector of old VWs; eight or nine

Who could resist an original paint '67 Bus just sitting in the weeds? Steve Sanchez dragged this one home in 2008, and it soon found a new owner. This would be an epic find today. (Courtesy Steve Sanchez)

years ago he found around 15-30 Split Buses and Trucks over a one or two year period and dragged many of them home. Some of these Buses were sold to fund others, some were built into Patina drivers, with

VW guys love old 'VW Group' cars and vans too, such as this 1957 DKW/ Auto Union Schnellaster that Steve recently rescued. (Courtesy Steve Sanchez)

Steve's current '65 Beetle as it was discovered – it may look like a great basis, but it took a few months to carry out the body-off preservation type restoration. (Courtesy Steve Sanchez)

A Titian Red & Beige Grey Split Westy in this condition would be an amazing find in this day and age. Steve Sanchez rescued this one back in 2008 when they were a bit easier to find for not a lot of money. (Courtesy Steve Sanchez)

the help of Steve's buddy Craig Yelley – if you've read *Patina Volkswagens* then you'll be familiar with Craig's work through his company Vintage VW in Spokane.

Steve got to a point where there were no Split Buses left to find, and he took a break from hunting – major life changes also put a block on things for a while. More recently though, Steve is back out hunting and finding Bugs and Buses – he's recently dragged a lot of early Bay Window Buses home, and a few mid-'60s Beetles too. He's just finished building a lovely original paint '65 Beetle with Craig's help; the chances are he

would have passed up on this car a few years ago as it wasn't early or rare enough for him, or he'd have sold it to someone in Europe or in an area of the USA where a '65 Beetle in good original condition was already a big deal.

As time goes on, people's viewpoints are changing and different years and models of VWs are becoming desirable when they wouldn't have seemed like a big deal two, five, ten, or 20 years ago. I like to think of this as a change of perspective – if you took a picture with an iPhone 3 ten years ago, you'd have been pretty amazed at the quality of the picture. Now if someone sends you a picture from an iPhone 3, though, it would be of laughable quality: with iPhones 6, 7, 8 and

Not all of Steve's discoveries have been restorable, but he either sells them to someone with the skills and inclination to put them back on the road, or they are a valuable source of parts for other restorations. (Courtesy Steve Sanchez)

Purchased by me in 2003 for just $3000, this all original '63 Double Cab had been off the road since the early '70s, had very little rust and was mostly complete. A similar find would be upwards of $25000 in the current climate. (Author's collection)

Dennis Pecchenino was lucky to be in the right place at the right time to score these two original paint beauties; quite often people get very attached to cars and struggle to let them go. (Courtesy Dennis Pecchenino)

In years gone by, when a Bus like this would cost $3000, it was worth taking an educated risk. Nowadays it'd cost at least five times that figure, so it's a much bigger gamble to buy sight unseen. (Courtesy Broos Defrancq)

beyond, the pictures are insane quality and resolution in comparison to older models, so people's standards and perspectives have changed. The supply of VWs has done a similar thing.

Obviously, the great thing about someone like Steve is that he has taken a lot of the back road journeys to find VWs and put in the legwork with owners. I'd also be willing to hazard a guess that he's left his number with a good few people who will call him if they ever find an old VW – as far as they're concerned, he's the VW guy! I'm pretty sure that Steve's current run of car and Bus finds is no fluke, he likely remembers all of the Bay Window Buses and '60s Bugs that were in people's yards – some of them may have even been sitting alongside Split Buses that Steve extracted years ago. Don't envy Steve – he's put in the hours, served his time, and has a great network as a result.

When you think about it, owning and driving an old VW, and doing what it takes to keep it on the road, is quite a commitment – the repair and maintenance of these cars is beyond the scope of anyone who doesn't want to take the time to learn. Some would say that to drive an old VW on a daily basis is a hardship or a sacrifice: poor demisting, crude heating system, slow, noisy, no A/C, etc. This is especially true if you are used to the comforts of a modern car, or cover a lot of miles every week. As the decades have gone on, cars have become bigger, more refined, more economical, and much faster. Whilst it is still possible to drive an air-cooled VW every day, it does mean sacrificing some of those modern refinements.

It's for these very reasons that other see people like Steve, who drive their old VWs often, as opposed to keeping them locked away like a toy to use occasionally, as different to the norm. Imagine having an old VW or ten sitting outside your house and then

imagine how many times people would be knocking on your door asking to buy the car or cars. Most of the people would be in a discreet modern vehicle; you'd probably think that they can make a profit on the internet from your car, and you'd mistrust their intentions. Now think for a minute if the person knocking at the door was driving an old, beaten-up but clearly loved and cherished VW, similar to the type of car you had outside. I believe that you'd likely trust their intentions a bit more and be more inclined to let them have a look.

Of course, it's often not quite this simple if you want to become the new owner of a car that someone has owned for literally decades: maybe they never intended to let it sit for that long? We've all heard people say that they don't want to sell something because they are going to restore it someday, and then it just sits for ten more years, but often people are, quite rightly, sentimentally attached to these cars, and have really never thought about selling. They are probably sick of the attention and feel like they have a right to privacy – many people don't like anyone trespassing on their property, and this includes cold callers at the front door – so you'd need to tread carefully, maybe leave a hand-written note about the car first, then follow up with a visit a few days later.

Some people will never sell anything – they'll keep it until the day they die, then the executor of the estate will have to deal with it, but for others, the timing may not be right to sell when you first approach. Often a specific event in people's lives makes them want to get rid of stuff or simplify their lives, and there's no guarantee when or if it will happen. Although you may want to buy the car, if they flatly refuse to sell it, you could offer to help them get it back on the road – this kind offer may eventually net you the car, but it may not; you should only offer to do this from a place of kindness – being happy to help out a fellow VW guy (or girl) – and be determined to see your promise through: it's good karma. Leastways, you might end up with another VW friend and a great story to tell.

Of course, not everyone is able to spend the time driving back roads; for these people, it's a matter of putting out feelers and checking sites like Craigslist every day – there are still cars springing up all the time, especially if you love **all** VWs and would be happy with a Patina ride from the 1970s; the later model cars, especially in the USA, were always unfashionable in the VW scene, so there are plenty still lying around. In Europe and countries where the good '60s cars dried up a long time ago, 1970s Volkswagens have been popular for many years – supply and demand kicking in once again.

This '64 Mouse Grey Bus was sold to me as having solid sills and being original paint. When it turned up it had pop-riveted sills and had been repainted. Fortunately, a Bus like this wasn't too much money in 2013, so some tribute logos were added for a bit of fun. (Author's collection)

When local isn't an option

If, like me, you live in the UK, you can only dream of finding great Patina cars on your doorstep, and really, the only way you're going to find cars is to visit dry areas, or find cars through the internet or social media. One of the best ways to have cars and parts pop up on your radar is to have a large social media network – follow people who are into VWs in these drier areas and befriend them. If possible, once you've got to know them, you can approach them personally and tell them you're looking to buy, or post on your timeline that you're looking to buy something specific; the wider your network, the better chance you have of a social media friend – or one of their friends – having something that might be just what you're looking for.

Outside of social media, sites like thesamba.com are the best option for finding good cars. People from all over the world advertise on there, so you may find your dream project car has already been imported to your country by someone and is literally for sale around the corner. If not, then buying a car overseas is an option you should entertain – it's not for everyone and there's a degree of trust and patience involved, but it may mean you can pick up a car cheaper than you could locally.

The downsides of importing from another country come with the appraisal and buying processes, and the fact that, while a picture does paint a thousand words, it can also be deceiving. I've lost count of the amount of VWs I've personally imported from overseas and, although I'm a seasoned buyer and can take an educated guess on the condition of a car from pictures and description, there are always surprises with every single purchase when it finally arrives after a lengthy shipping process.

Buying a car overseas – appraisal

Using the internet or social media to buy a car overseas counts on a lot of trust; 99 per cent of people will never take a flight overseas to check out a car in person, or pay a local appraiser to do it for them. This is pretty understandable, as both of these would add to the already significant cost of buying and paying an expensive shipping bill. Without inspecting a car, or meeting the owner, you're putting yourself at risk of losing all your money, never receiving the vehicle, receiving a wreck, or a car with missing parts. Having imported numerous cars over nearly 20 years, I've experienced all of these things to some degree.

What these experiences taught me to do was to imagine a worst case scenario with the car that you're seeing in pictures, and thinking about whether you'd still buy it; what if the small rust bubble you can see on the rocker panel is actually more serious in real life, and the panel needs to be completely replaced? What if the owner is lying when he says there is no rust in the sills/rockers, and the inner panel is completely rusted away, or it wasn't fitted when someone chose to fit an outer panel to make it look good?

What if the car doesn't match the paperwork, or the body is just sitting on the wrong year floorpan and none of the numbers matches the title document?

I chose to buy this one sight unseen in 2005 and was rewarded with a great rust free Bus for $1000. Even if something seems like a bargain it's always worth getting lots of pictures and doing your best to figure out if the vendor is trustworthy.
(Author's collection)

What if you buy a Bus that's titled and described as a '75, but when it arrives it's been 'ringed' – it's a '77 Bus with the VIN plate from a '75 pop-riveted over the cut out original numbers? What if you buy a 1970 Bus that has no ID or VIN numbers anywhere? These are all real-life scenarios. Some of these issues would get picked up by a shipper, some would go undetected until you tried to register your project when you've spent thousands of hours and a huge sum of money on the build. How does the cost of an airline ticket, or a local appraiser look now?

Sending money overseas

Apart from escrow services, where a third party keeps the money until the buyer is satisfied, there really is no secure way to send money as a buyer and be protected. There's also very little likelihood of a vendor being happy to accept escrow, especially as it will often be months until you receive a car through a shipper – they could have the money instantly with a local buyer. They could also argue that you could lie about the condition of the car upon arrival, which is true.

Having said that, sending money via a bank wire at least gives you a verified name and address in case you need to try to get your money back in the future – you wouldn't get this with something like Western Union. PayPal is now more secure than it used to be, but the PayPal disputes system can be open to abuse by unscrupulous people – their buyer protection also doesn't apply for vehicle deposits.

Finding an appraiser vs jumping on a plane

Finding someone who knows what they are looking at to appraise a car for you is easier in some areas than others – places like Southern California are a hotbed of VW activity and have a lot of reputable VW shops and specialists. Many specialists may not offer appraisal services on their website, but if you contact them, then they may be able to help out for a fee. Failing this, you may be able to put out a post on social media to get help, or contact people you know on social media in the area.

Bear in mind that you're relying on their expertise, but what they see is still very open to interpretation – they may not spot something that you would, or be as thorough. Similarly, getting an airline ticket and heading over to see a potential purchase may be a complete waste of time and money if the car turns out to be literally junk – it would save you thousands by not buying into a potential nightmare, but would still be costly and would come out of your budget. These are all things to consider when thinking about appraising vs buying sight unseen.

Buying sight unseen

The way I like to approach buying VWs sight unseen is this: get lots of pictures and information via email and/or phone calls – pictures of usual problem areas are a necessity. If they aren't forthcoming, then walk away, unless it's too cheap to pass up. If a car seems way too cheap to not buy instantly, then question why it is cheap. Is the person advertising the car even the owner? Are they trying to scam people? There are literally hundreds of different scams about, so be very careful. Always question the seller about getting the car inspected, and if they come up with excuses, walk away.

Buying a project, like my most recent purchase, without getting detailed pictures from the vendor would be stupid at best; even if it was cheap, you can bet the shipping would cost a pretty penny if you're not local. (Courtesy Adam 'EMPI GT' Cunningham)

If you're buying a car that someone else has already built, then ask for build pictures – most people take lots of build and restoration pics these days, so if they aren't available, then ask why not – buying a 'done' car with shoddy workmanship that needs to be completely redone is another thing that happens every day. What's more, in countries or areas where there are no annual or bi-annual roadworthiness inspections, people can build shoddy cars without their work being ever called into question.

Could I sell and recoup my money?

One question I always ask myself when buying any car from overseas is: "What's the current market value for this car in my country." Even if you have no intention of selling the car now, or at any point in the future, knowing that what you're paying for the car could be recouped if necessary, or if it was in worse condition than you expected, at least gives you an airbag – some peace of mind that you're not throwing your money away.

Shipping a vehicle

Depending on which country you're buying the car from, overland transport can usually be found on uship.com or shiply.com. If you're looking into ocean freight and are UK based, then Kingstown Shipping (www.kingstownshipping. co.uk) come highly recommended – they can

Having your shipping logistics figured out before you spot a dream purchase can pay dividends; most vendors are wary of selling to overseas buyers, so having all your ducks in a row helps to build confidence, as well as being able to act fast. (Author's collection)

Sometimes a gamble pays off; I bought this '72 Bus for $400 back in 2007. The shipping cost was around £1500 on top but the one picture convinced me that it was a solid, original paint Bus. (Author's collection)

Although to many this would just be a worthless pile of junk, I knew that this '51 Bus was worth almost ten times the £500 it cost to buy. (Author's collection)

usually handle the whole process from start to finish to the UK or Europe. It's also worth asking around on social media or internet forums for recommendations; I've used several shippers over the years, but, for one reason or another, can only recommend one.

Before even considering sending money overseas for a car, it would be wise to get a detailed quote for shipping based on the size and country/year of manufacture. This should include not only the ocean freight costs, but also the loading, unloading and destination charges, as well as the cost for paperwork and customs clearance. Some companies will require this to be paid in advance, whereas others will accept 'collect payment' (once the vehicle arrives at the destination). Collect payment can give you more time to save the funds for shipping, especially if you buy a car at the top end of your budget.

Quite often pictures will only tell you part of the story; it's a good idea to assume that any rust goes further than you can see in the pictures. Of course, if you're a seasoned restorer, rust like this won't be a deal-breaker. (Courtesy Adam 'EMPI GT' Cunningham)

Documentation

If you're buying a car to ship overseas from the USA, or other countries, you will need a title document for the vehicle – you can't ship a car without one. Title documents can be applied for by a shipper, but this usually costs around $400-500 and can take up to eight weeks. If buying a car in Europe, paperwork is also necessary in most cases, depending on which country you're going to be registering it in – some countries have more stringent regulations and more red tape than others.

Buying – what to look out for

Although, when it comes to old cars, everything costs a significant amount of money to repair or replace, there's never anything more costly than rebuilding rusted, accident damaged, or poorly repaired bodywork. I understand that, if you're buying a 'finished' car, then it clearly helps if everything is up to scratch, but the best advice I can give is to buy the best body you can – everything else is of secondary concern. Although there are several body repair specialists around who do amazing quality metal repair, this is a very time-consuming and costly process to do right.

For every one person who does great metal repair, there are 1000 who do average or poor work, so it's easy to buy a car that looks right, only to find issues lurking under the paint – this is why completely original cars, even with rust repair needed, are favourable to restored cars. The fact is, no one ever knows how well a car has been restored until it is stripped back to the metal. It's for this reason that this section about what to look out for when buying will only cover the floorpan and body: the metal.

As well as reading this section on body appraisal, it helps to be aware of the current cost – and rarity – of any missing parts. A quick Google search or a search in the classifieds section of thesamba.com will tell you if the missing parts are easy to find or not. If you just have to have good original upholstery over new, then you'd be wise to buy a car with this to begin with – make a list of all of the 'must-haves' for your project car and try not to be swayed by a cool looking car that doesn't tick many things on your list.

Floorpan cars – buying

The pictures in this section will show problem areas for the bodywork and floorpan of the cars not of monocoque construction – Beetle, Karmann Ghia, Type 3, and Type 181. With these cars, it's always best to remove the body from the floorpan to carry out any rust repair or restoration work. Truth be told, a large

Getting detailed pictures from a vendor may not give you 100 per cent of the picture of car condition, but it acts as damage limitation at least. (Courtesy Daniel Mandat)

It's safe to assume that most Bugs, even those from a fairly dry climate, will need the floorpan halves replaced. In general, it's body rust that is harder to repair. (Courtesy Daniel Mandat)

majority of cars will need the floorpans repaired or replaced. Floorpan replacement is actually quite a simple job – it requires welding skills, but is not as specialist as carrying out invisible butt-welded repairs to bodywork, for example.

Of course, it's not just the floorpan halves themselves that rust, but anywhere and everywhere on the floorpan structure – lower frame head, lower spine, and lots of other localised areas. Depending on how bad the structure of the floorpan is, some people choose to replace the whole pan with that from another car. The issue when doing this is that the VIN number will be different on the replacement pan, and changing ID by welding in one from another pan

There's no substitute for removing all of the original carpets to assess the condition of the body metal – unfortunately it's not always possible when buying from a distance. (Courtesy Jason Reich)

Original paint on the heater channels is always a good sign, but there's still the possibility they'll be rusted underneath – unlike Jason Reich's immaculate Bug. (Courtesy Jason Reich)

Rear package tray rust is very common, usually due to a leaking rear window rubber. The problem is, most cars have carpet covering this area, so it's hard to appraise, especially in pictures. (Courtesy Daniel Mandat)

is illegal in some countries or areas. This is why it's important to check that all the numbers match when buying.

Body

When it comes to checking out the body of a prospective purchase, you're not only looking for rust, but also accident damage, or evidence of any past repairs. Whilst we're going to look at common areas for rust and body damage here, practically any area of the body can have damage, or have been repaired in the past. Cars from wetter climates, coastal areas, and places where road salt is used, can have bodies in worse condition than those from dry, inland regions.

If you're a good welder, then you may be tempted by these rustier cars and that's up to you, but just be aware that, when you weld up a cavity section, the metal inside the cavity will oxidise as you are welding and you'll never be able to fully eradicate this rust. It's for this very reason, that it's always better to find as dry and rust-free a car as you can afford. By far the most complicated and expensive area to repair on these separate floorpan cars are heater channels, and it's really easy to do a poor repair. In order to access the inside of the heater channels, adjoining front bulkhead and rear crossmember (under the back seat), it will be necessary to remove some carpets and trim. This isn't always possible, however, so you may have to be guided by the condition of the outer and surrounding metal.

When you're looking at the heater channels, the first place to look is underneath – the bottom plates are just under where the running boards mount on Bugs, and should have all of the factory pressings still visible. If they don't, then this area has been patched or replaced with flat steel. The area behind the running boards and the inner door shut area should also look right – comparing it to pictures of cars that are original will help you to figure out if you're looking at factory original steel.

It's not uncommon for the running board mounting area and door shut areas to be repaired with patch panels. This can be done correctly by cutting out the original metal and butt-welding in a good repair panel,

but many people choose (or did choose back in the '80s and '90s) to just weld the panel over the rusted original part, and make good with filler or Bondo. Once you've finished investigating these panels, take a look at the bulkhead area under the fuel tank: this will often rust in the corners, and is a body-off job to repair correctly.

The front valance/apron is the next place to check, as well as rusted-out bumper mounts on the inner wings, this area is prone to rust and accident damage. Checking if the bonnet/hood lines up correctly is also a tell-tale sign of old accident damage. The seal channel area on the inner wings and scuttle panel is prone to rust because the seals trap moisture, and the lower front A-panels – where they attach to the heater channels – can visibly show rust in the small triangle area behind the front wing/fender.

Looking under the wing/fender here, you should be able to see original factory pressings and spot welds – at the factory, the inner wing was actually spot welded to the heater channel around 1-2in from the bottom, but the available repair sections are usually a cover-all and include the lower body lip too – if your car has been repaired this way, then it'll make fixing it correctly more time-consuming and the patch/cover panel could have trapped more rust, causing it to rust out even more underneath the poor repair.

Moving to the rear inner wings, it's common for the rear body mounts to rust – this is a multi-layered panel, so the vast majority of people just cut off the top layer of metal and weld a patch panel over the top. In order to repair this area properly, the factory spot welds need to be drilled out and both the inner and outer panels may need repair (the inner part will be covered by the original carpet). While you're inside peeling back the carpets, it's also worth trying to access the rear boot/trunk floor, and the area under the rear window. This area can be particularly vulnerable to rust, as the rear window rubber will have perished and cracked over the years, allowing rainwater to leak in undetected.

Finally, at least as far as structural bodywork, the rear bumper mounts are a common corrosion area, especially as dirt is thrown up from the rear wheels and trapped in the corner where the wing/fender mounts to the body, which is also the bumper mounting area. This is another multi-layered area when it comes to repairing, but very good quality body panels are available at least. When it comes down to it, any area can be repaired on a Bug body, either by using body cuts from another car, or widely available repair panels. The only thing you need to consider on a Patina car is how easy is it going to be to match the repaired areas to the original paint.

Karmann Ghia, Type 3, and Type 181/Trekker/Thing

When it comes to these models, although they are also separate floorpan cars, the repair panels are nowhere near as widely available as they are for a Bug or Bus. When it comes to body repair on these models, you'll be more reliant on buying good body cuts to repair any rust or damage or using metal shaping skills to make your own panels for complex areas. All of these types of VW can and do rust really badly, and it can be pretty well hidden – the Karmann Ghia models are coach-built, so you can't even remove the wings/fenders to inspect for rust, or to afford better access for repairs.

When it comes to appraising the Type 3 and other floorpan cars, they can literally rust anywhere – if you don't know your way around these cars, you'll save yourself a lot of money and heartache by getting someone who *does* know to look over the car before

It's especially important to ensure that a Type 3 has little body rust; most panels are unavailable currently, unless

At least the wings on Type 3 models are removable, making rust repair a little easier. The same cannot be said for Karmann Ghia models though. (Courtesy Sublime Classic Restorations /Gareth Bayliss-Smith)

you buy it. Contrary to popular belief, even California cars rust, and there are very few truly 'rust-free' cars out there any more. Luckily though, there are more repair panels around for the Ghias and Type 3s than there used to be – people like Gerson at Klassicfab have tooled up to make so many repair sections that just weren't available five or ten years ago, and one of these panels is good quality floorpan halves for the Type 3 models. Heater channels and outer sill panels are also available.

Fortunately for Type 3 owners, Gerson at Klassicfab now manufactures good replacement floorpans. (Courtesy Sublime Classic Restorations/Gareth Bayliss-Smith)

Type 2 – Bay Window and Split Screen Buses

Unlike the Beetle, and other models with a separate floorpan, the Bus production models were always a one-piece monocoque construction for strength – Volkswagen tried a separate floorpan on the Bus in the prototype stage, but it just wasn't strong enough. Both early and late models of the Bus had strong chassis rails, which are tied into the body structure by a series of outriggers that are welded to the inner sill panels.

Buses rust, and they rust bad, but it's possible to repair if you have reasonably good welding and fabricating skills. The main problem with Buses, as with all other models, is when they've already been got at by someone who should have known better, or repaired before good quality repair panels were available. The main structure of a Bus is fairly complex, and carrying out a repair properly – even to a

The only positive to be taken from a picture like this, is that the Bus hasn't been poorly repaired in the past. Whilst time-consuming, this really isn't too difficult to repair, especially with the current availability of high-quality repair panels. (Courtesy Adam 'EMPI GT' Cunningham)

Being of unitary construction, it's not as easy to repair the underside of a Bus as it is with a Beetle. (Courtesy Adam 'EMPI GT' Cunningham)

Good pictures of the outriggers and jack points are helpful when appraising a Bus. There's still the possibility that they will be packed full of wet, sandy dirt, though. (Courtesy Adam 'EMPI GT' Cunningham)

A picture like this says a thousand words. Whilst some may find this off-putting, it at least shows quite a few different areas. This could be called typical Bus rust these days. (Courtesy Adam 'EMPI GT' Cunningham)

small area – can involve repairing several small panels, but if you're patient and put in the correct research, you can repair the body of a Bus correctly.

On Buses that have had a pretty blessed life, the most common places to find rust are in the front floors and the battery tray; even really dry Buses can have rust here, due to the driver and passengers climbing in with wet feet, the original rubber floor mats holding condensation and moisture against the metal, and, in the case of the battery tray, battery acid leaking and causing the panel to rust out from above. These are the first areas to look at on an apparently dry Bus, as well as the lower rear corners adjacent to the battery trays on both sides.

The next most common area to rust on Buses is the sills/rockers. On Split Buses it's a simple inner and outer, although the cargo door sill/rocker also has an inner strengthener. On Bay Window Buses the sills are in three parts: inner, centre, and outer. These panels include a cavity section that can trap dirt and moisture inside, this being held against the metal for long periods of time is what normally causes these panels to rust from the inside out. Trapped mud underneath a Bus won't do them any favours either.

Depending on how rusty the Bus you're looking at is, you may just be faced with some small rust bubbles on the outer sill, or you may be faced with a Bus where the whole sill has rusted so badly that there's virtually nothing left – rust will also continue further into the structure of the Bus, affecting the jacking points, outriggers, supporting top hats, and I section floor supporting beams. When the rust gets this bad, there will also be rust damage to the inner front wheel wells at the front end of the sill and the rear wheel well closing panels at the rear end. All panels are available to repair the sills/rockers, and the panels are so good

Both battery trays are prone to rusting on Buses, as well as the engine bay side trays and rear corners. By the glimmer of daylight in this picture, it's also safe to assume that the inner wheelwell will need some repairs. (Courtesy Adam 'EMPI GT' Cunningham)

that, if repaired by a skilled repairer, you won't be able to tell that they have been done.

Next on the hit list for Buses that have had a more average life, are the front and rear wheelarches – outer panels are available, or whole panels if the rust has gone further. The inner and outer lower front valance is also a cavity section and can rust badly, as can the area underneath the windscreen/windshield – often with the latter, you may not be able to tell if the lower window channel has rusted through until you remove the glass and sealing rubber. Dried out, perished, and shrunken rubber are tell-tale signs of trapped moisture, as cracks in the seals can let in water; ironically, in some hotter countries, where the rubbers perish like this, the rust underneath the window rubbers can be much worse than in a colder climate.

In some cases, especially where there has been a pop-top roof fitted, or where a Bus has been allowed to sit for years with leaves and other debris in the roof gutters, these can rust out really badly; it's a complicated area to repair, as the gutters and roof edge are formed in several sections. Generally, roof edge rust is reserved for Buses on the really bad end of the spectrum, but I've also seen Buses that are really dry low down, but have suffered in this area due to rodents making a bed in the cant rail inside the roof, or due to '70s camper conversions where someone has used fibreglass type insulation, which soaks up moisture like a sponge and holds it against the roof.

As I said previously, any area of an air-cooled VW can (and does) rust, and, while there are typical areas, no old car rusts exactly the same as another car, even of the same model and year. If you're not an expert on the ins and outs of old VWs and how they rust, then you won't know how to look out for signs that

No matter how much you think you know about a project vehicle by looking at pictures, there'll always be a few surprises when it arrives. (Author's collection)

something may be amiss, or if something has been repaired badly. In this case, you should always think about taking a professional, or at least professional VW hobbyist along for the inspection. Whilst no real substitute for experience, spending a few months checking out people's restoration and build threads on forums, such as those on thesamba.com, will show you how certain areas are supposed to look and how panels were welded together at the factory.

The bottom line is that, depending on how well it's appraised, it could save you a lot of money or cost you a lot of money to put right – bear this in mind when you're struggling to justify the cost of paying a professional to appraise a potential purchase or funding an airline ticket to check out a potential car. Taking the time and money now to get forewarning of any potential problems will also help you to plan your project and budget for any extra parts or work should you decide to go ahead and purchase the car regardless.

CHAPTER THREE
Stripdown & parts ordering

It's quite an exciting time when the body finally comes off a project car; it's the only way to properly repair rusted floorpans or lower bodywork on a Beetle, Karmann Ghia, Type 3 or Type 181.
(Courtesy Gareth Bayliss-Smith)

Although a pre-purchase check and appraisal will give you some idea of the condition of your base vehicle, it will only become apparent just how much work is needed when it is stripped of ancillary parts. Even on cars where a rolling restoration is needed, there are steps that need to be taken to ascertain vehicle condition before parts can be ordered.

So, you've followed the book so far and you've been lucky enough to score a cool Patina VW project car, and managed to get it shipped to your front door. When this happens, you may be able to jump in full steam ahead on a project, or you may be limited to grabbing the odd few hours or days to work on the car between work and family commitments. Whatever your limitations when it comes to tackling a project, there's no doubt that if you carve out a time to work on it often, then you'll be making progress, no matter how small.

Project cars and frustration

The number one reason that projects stall and cars get sold is that owners look at the entire build as one huge job and one massive undertaking. My buddy Johnny works away from home all week, every week and has a wife and small child at home to occupy his time when he gets home on weekends. Despite having virtually no time to work on his project cars, he carves out a small opportunity each weekend – sometimes it may just be ten minutes to clean or paint something, other times he may get lucky and manage an hour before everyone else wakes up. The point I'm making is that rarely can you make the excuse that you don't get time. You have to make time if it's something that's important to you.

The thing is, Johnny often gets irritated at such baby steps of progress, but his mantra "little and often gets it done" is true. He recently didn't find the time to carve out even ten minutes each weekend and, sure enough, after a few weeks of this, he was talking about selling all of his cars. I think it was when I pointed

Johnny Montana started his full Patina build back in 2012 – he's at seven years and counting, but most importantly progress is still being made. This was the day I went to the docks with Johnny and his wife, Lucy, to collect the car after its trip from Arkansas, USA. (Author's collection)

Johnny's Beetle has a lovely Patina fade on the original Gulf Blue paint. The car is undergoing a full body-off Patina build with clearcoated body. (Author's collection)

out how far he'd come with his project at just his little and often rate, he realised that his project was about 10,000 per cent closer to completion than it would be if he was still waiting to find the time. Realising that a project is less of a whole cake to eat and more a series of small bites is what separates the guys who successfully build car after car, from the ones who seem to keep a car for a few months (or years) with little progress, then get fed up and sell.

The number two reason for projects stalling and cars getting sold is poor planning: you need to plan ahead to try to have the correct parts waiting for you when you undertake a certain job, otherwise you'll jack it in after ten minutes with no forward progress and, after a few times of this you might think "I can't do this" and be tempted to sell to someone who can. Having worked on old Volkswagens my entire adult life, I can tell you that they're pretty simple to work on and "I can't" is just an excuse, or because you can't be bothered to spend the time to learn, or to figure out a problem – it's definitely not brain surgery and you may make a few mistakes while trying, but as long as you make sure safety features are checked by someone competent, then you can't go very far wrong.

Bulk-buy consumables

Add being on a tight budget to the equation and your planning ahead will have another obstacle in the way, but there are thousands of 'free' jobs you can do on a project when you maybe can't afford the parts to progress fully with one area of the build – there's always something to clean, something to sand, some paint to strip, or a small component to restore or paint. The best thing to do at the start of any project is to 'cry once' and try to bulk-buy black paint, primer, wet and dry paper, degreaser, brushes, gloves, and any other consumables for the job at hand – you might be shocked at the bill for 20 cans of paint, some sandpaper, and cleaning chemicals, but if you have zero money to spend in the middle of the month and the lack of having one can of gloss black paint or primer, or the lack of a box of gloves, is holding up the entire project, then it's eventually going to hit your morale levels hard.

There was a time that materials, paint, and chemicals were pretty cheap to buy and you almost didn't need to factor the cost into the job, but nowadays these kind of things are much more expensive, so if you ignore or forget about materials and just think about the cost of the project car and the parts, then you're missing out on planning for at least 20-30 per cent of the final build cost.

Bulk-buying things like this, putting everything

away, and working tidily will alert you early on that you're low on paint: before you're working on the car on a Sunday afternoon when the paint store is closed, or before your wife takes the shared car to meet her friends and you realise you need to get across town to buy something. Putting this in a how-to book seems a little ridiculous, but things like this get overlooked and cause delays and frustration.

Clean everything first

With the materials and consumables fully stocked, the next stage is to assess what you've bought and the best way to do this is to thoroughly clean everything you can get to before you even start to dismantle anything – some forward-thinking individuals spend a productive hour at the jet wash when the car is still on the trailer – en route from where you bought it from, or when you picked it up from the shipping warehouse. This is one reason that renting a trailer and going to pick up your own project car is a good idea: if it's a non-runner, and maybe even hard to push around, with flat tyres etc you will be glad you took the opportunity to wash the car – inside and out – whilst the car was still on the trailer.

Whether you have access to a jet wash on the way home or not, the very first thing you should do when a new project car arrives is to give everything a thorough clean. Depending on your storage situation – not everyone has the luxury of dry indoor storage – you may wish to leave all of the glass in your car, so it's watertight until you're ready to change the window rubbers on a dry summer's day. Whatever you decide with respect to the glass, the first and best thing to do is to wash the car inside and out – if you have cloth interior parts, carefully remove and store the interior panels, seats and other interior parts before giving the whole inside a thorough wash out with several buckets full of hot, soapy water.

For reasons that will soon be clear, you'll need thick waterproof gloves, a particle/dust/filtered mask for this stage, as well as some safety glasses. It also helps to have a kneeling pad so you can keep yourself reasonably clean as you begin the cleaning process – as you don't know what has been living in your project car and what hazards they've left behind, it helps to be aware of your surroundings and take precautions against things such as rodent droppings which can literally be deadly if particles are inhaled.

Whilst you're removing the interior to access and clean the interior metal and painted areas, have a running list going – a piece of paper taped to a window and a pen close by is handy here – don't think "I'll make a mental list" as you're likely to miss something. List

Taking your project to a local car wash before you bring it home, or after you've stripped out the interior, can save a lot of time and effort. Here, I wash a new project inside, outside, and underneath.
(Author's collection)

any parts that are broken, where you need to source replacements, or even if you need to source small parts to repair or replace – things like the correct screws for lights and lenses often go missing and are replaced with generic screws and bolts; a rusty countersink wood screw will stand out a mile on a finished car.

Once any perishable items, like cloth upholstery, have been removed, you can begin the cleaning process – it's likely if you're starting with a junkyard car, or one that has been stored (either inside or outside) for years or decades that you will have spider's webs, wasp nests, and rodent droppings/rodent bedding, or even a few small critters, to deal with. Use thick black bin bags to bag up all of the mess, and use a vacuum cleaner rather than a brush if possible – it would probably help to buy a cheap vacuum cleaner that you'll use solely for project cars and empty it regularly.

One thing to mention: Don't throw any parts away until you have sourced a replacement! You may think the rubber floor mats, or other parts, are

Even after a project car goes through the car wash, there will still be days of cleaning ahead, especially as you remove more parts. (Author's collection)

Cleaning up and restoring parts as you take them off is one preferred way to do it; at least then they'll be ready when you need them. (Author's collection)

too sorry to be re-used, but you'll likely change your mind if you can't source better replacements, or you find out that the part you took to the dump is a rare, one-year-only part that's unobtainable.

Work out a plan

You may think that there's only one way to tackle a project car, but you'd be wrong. Lots of people choose to strip a car and tackle all of the welding and paint repairs first, for instance, then restore all the small parts and running gear later. The trouble with this is that you'll mentally feel like you're nearly done with the project once the car is a rust-free shell with all of the paint repairs completed. I've lost count of the people I know who have stalled with a project when this happens, as they suddenly realise they are only 50 per cent of the way through the project.

Conversely, the people who restore all of the small components and running gear first, then are faced with diving into all of the body repairs and paintwork after this can also stall; maybe this is because they were putting off the metalwork as a 'big job' – seeing it as replacing all of the rusty metal, rather than a series of smaller welded repairs. I like to think of rust repair like a big cake – you can see it as having to get through the whole cake, or you can see it as a series of smaller slices; each smaller slice can also be divided into a series of smaller bites. Rust repair is the same – it should be seen as a series of smaller jobs; each job can also be completed in several sessions, so even if you only have 30 minutes to spare, you can still move the job along.

Middle ground

I'll go on the record and say I've always been in the former camp, especially with bigger projects – I know that if I don't tackle the metal repairs first, that I'll continue putting the work off. Although I've learned to do good quality metal repairs over the years, it's still not something I actively enjoy doing – I like seeing the results of a nice metal finished repair, but find the actual work a chore – pick the jobs that you dislike or will put off the most and do them first!

This huge bowl of rat poison was spotted in a '69 Bay-window Bus whilst collecting a project from the shipping port; rodents and their droppings are a real risk factor when tackling Patina projects, especially junkyard cars, or those that have been sitting in the wilderness for years. (Author's collection)

Having said all of this, I think that making a solid time plan of when you'll do specific jobs, means that you'll carry them out in a complementary manner: you'll do them in the order that you want the project to run in. Want to build up a Beetle floorpan completely before you set the body back on it? Then you'll need to start thinking about refurbishing the running gear as you weld in new floorpans, so that parts are ready once the pan is completed. This way, you can complete the whole 'pan, then cover it, and set it aside knowing it's all done.

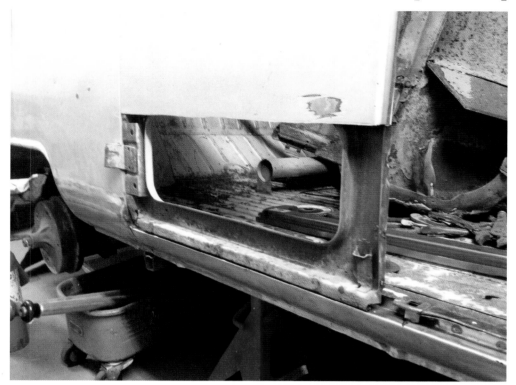

I have always preferred to carry out the metal repairs first on my projects, followed by paint and re-assembly. Restoring small parts as you go along can break up the monotony. (Author's collection)

Setting a deadline will likely make you rush certain aspects of the job; I set a deadline with this Bus and ended up having to revisit some of the work, which is bad for morale. (Author's collection)

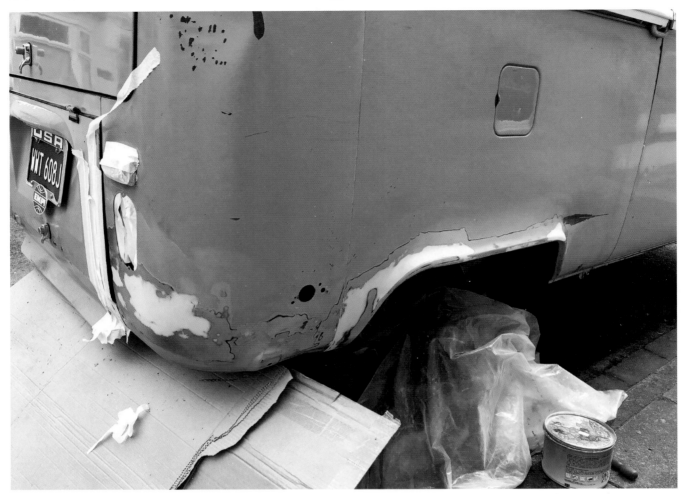

Carrying out any filling and bodywork after each area is repaired is a good way to break up the tunnel vision you can get into when carrying out all the metal repairs on a project. (Author's collection)

I have to say, despite having always completed all of the metalwork and paint on my projects before moving forward, I've more recently decided that a good balance to avoid getting sick of it, for me, is to do one day on metalwork, then take a break to rebuild something mechanical, or to sand and paint something. I find this the best balance for morale, and it avoids tunnel vision – emerging from the metalwork 'tunnel' feeling relieved, only to realise you have **everything** else to do isn't good for keeping positive. This is just my personal perspective from the experience of doing a lot of projects. I've also found that it's a good idea to do any filler work and fix bodywork on each repaired area first, before moving on – this breaks up one of the most monotonous parts of a vehicle restoration, as well as providing morale when each area looks more finished. It also means that you can apply primer to any bare metal areas before proceeding.

Think it through then times by four

Something else which comes up quite a lot is that when you are able to think through your project in its component form, you can often make the mistake of thinking that it will happen much quicker than it actually will. Even if you **know** that you can weld in both new floorpan halves in one day, quite often you'll get thrown a curveball: you'll find extra rust damage that will need addressing, will run out of welding gas, or your wife will call you to say she's ill and you need to look after the kids. These are all reasons why it's good to think through how long everything will take, but times it by four, then write it down on the plan. Look at it this way: if you finish a little sooner than you expect, you'll be a lot less frustrated than finishing much later.

Build some infrastructure

Before you dig into a new project, take some time to put

the necessary infrastructure in place, so that the project feels a lot easier. If you're lacking space in which to store parts correctly, then this will end up being a point of frustration, especially when you start to damage parts through improper or careless storage, or lose parts that you know you already have and have to spend out ordering them again. If you know you need to build a garage before you can easily do a project, then the time to do it is before you rip a car apart. Even something as simple as building some new shelves for storage, or clearing out some junk and selling old parts you no longer need will help you to feel on top of things.

Similarly, when it comes to tools, be prepared to invest in some good tool storage and prioritise spending money on some tools you know you'll need. When it comes to tools, the mantra is 'buy cheap, buy twice'; invest in quality tools that are backed by a warranty. Although nothing beats having your own tools, some tools can be rented for a fraction of the buying cost – things like spot welders and more specialist tools are usually available to rent locally. This is the kind of advice that sounds boring and maybe a little ridiculous, but to not do these things is to set yourself up to fail.

Bag and tag – be organised

Once you start to strip everything down, bagging and labelling each part and the fixings to hold it on will save you a lot of pain and guesswork later on – you'd be surprised how losing one screw or fixing will sideline you, or cost you dear when it comes to sourcing a replacement, both in terms of time and money – have you ever tried finding the correct domed nut to refit a pre '64 Bus rear hatch handle, or front door screws with the correct profile?

Bag and organise all parts in groups if possible – locks and latches in one box, window fittings in another, etc. Anything that won't fit in a bag should be labelled with masking tape. With some parts, such as rear pop out windows, you can either tape a bag with the screws in onto the glass, or fit the screws back into the frame for safekeeping; spending a few seconds here can save you hours (or weeks waiting for parts) when it comes to reassembly.

Even if a rust-free car, like this early Squareback, looks like an easy project, it'll still soak up a lot of time. If you know you'll lose motivation, carve out some big chunks of time to work on the car – the progress will spur you on for a while. (Author's collection)

Take as many pictures as you can throughout the stripdown; even if you think you'll remember things, it's good to have a point of reference later. Wiring pictures are especially important, and will save time upon re-assembly. (Author's collection)

Parts sourcing – new vs used

When it comes to sourcing parts, there are a few things to take into account, but there's one thing I need to mention before we go any further: a lot of the reproduction parts out there for sale are junk, or not fit for purpose. Since I began messing with classic VWs back in the early 1990s, there has always been a problem with quality in the aftermarket parts sector; in some ways it's getting better, and in others worse. There are several companies out there spending a lot of time in product development, making new parts by using original or NOS (New Old Stock) parts as a reference. In many cases, buying a new part now vs five years ago means you're more likely to get something good quality around 50 per cent of the time.

The main problem I've found is with rubber parts – even the so-called 'German quality' parts from some manufacturers perish and split within six months

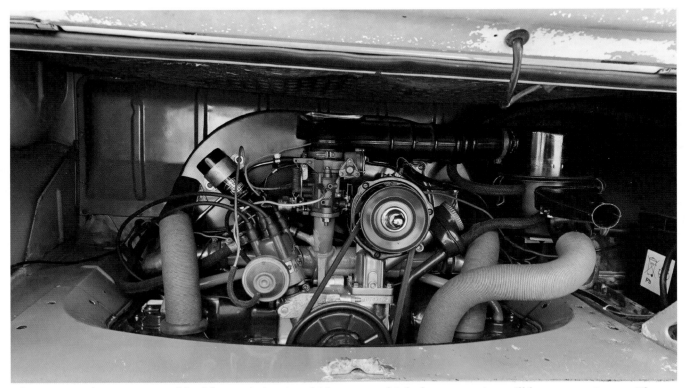

So many project cars are sold without engines, and it's easy to think that an engine will be easy to source. These days, finding a good used engine for sale is getting harder, and even when you do locate one, it can be difficult to find OEM quality ancillary parts to make it look correct. (Author's collection)

It's worth shopping around and, in some cases, paying extra for new parts, such as rubbers, trim, and mechanical items; there are some shocking quality parts around, so buy from a supplier who you trust and develop a relationship with them. (Author's collection)

Buses like this '66 Westy, which sat on the side of a mountain near the Canadian border for 30 years, will likely need most of the mechanical and rubber parts replaced. Where I would once replace everything as a matter of course, I now inspect each part and try to keep anything that is still serviceable – such is the quandary with the differing quality of new parts. (Author's collection)

of fitting. Having had all of the brand-new German quality ball joint rubbers split wide open on a 1973 Westfalia Camper I built a couple of years ago (the Bus was still being built and had driven zero miles), I must admit, now more than ever, I will often choose to assess an original, 40 plus-year-old Volkswagen part and, more often than not, re-use it.

In days gone by, I would replace **everything** when it came to brakes, suspension, steering, and controls; having been stung several times now, I will often inspect parts for wear and, if the part has plenty of life left in it, I will re-use it. This may sound backwards to most vehicle restorers, but unfortunately, it's just the way things are. In many cases, I would always recommend sourcing a good used part than a new one. If you do decide to buy new parts, go for the German quality or best quality parts and don't throw the old part away until you have compared it in size and likeness to the new one – you'd be surprised just how many new parts are nothing like the original, with many not fit for purpose.

Where to find parts

When it comes to sourcing original parts, websites like thesamba.com with its incredible searchable classifieds section will usually find you what you're looking for. Auction sites like eBay are also really useful, as is Facebook Marketplace. This is also where building a large network on social media will really help. Joining as many VW buy and sell groups as you can, as well as following lots of people in the VW scene is also great when you're looking for elusive original parts – you can also post wanted posts on social media, if all else fails. Junkyards or companies who stock used original parts are a great source of parts too, but bear in mind that they need to make a profit, so prices will often be higher than those being sold in a classified ad.

When it comes to new parts, it can really help to find one company that supplies quality products and build up a relationship with someone there – some of the smaller companies are better for this, as it's easy to feel like you're just a number to the larger parts suppliers. They also process so many orders each day, that it's unlikely they'll remember you if you call back later with a query or issue with something you've bought. If you find the right person and company to deal with, they'll be completely candid about the quality of the part you ask about and, in some cases, will tell you if it's worth ordering, or whether you'd be better to try and source an original or NOS part.

Fail to plan = plan to fail

When it comes down to it, how well you plan ahead before you take on a project will have an impact on how successful the outcome, and how stress-free the project unfolds. Don't forget, projects are

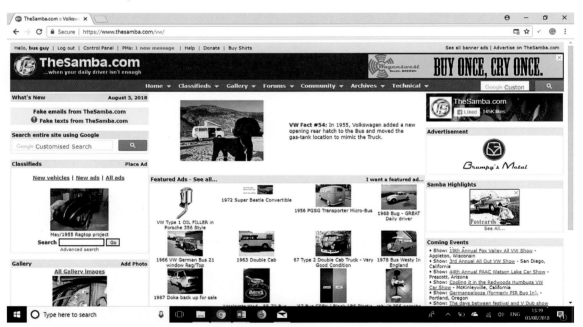

If you're looking for hard-to-find parts for your project, thesamba.com is a huge, worldwide marketplace – if you can't find a part on the searchable classifieds section, then you can place a wanted advert. Facebook Marketplace and eBay are also great hunting grounds.
(Courtesy Everett Barnes/thesamba.com)

supposed to be fun, so as much stress as you can limit or control will make doing the project so much more pleasurable; when it comes to projects, it's as much about the journey as the destination, so split the work down into easily-manageable tasks, and try not to put time pressures on yourself or the project completion date. When you begin to get in a time pinch, costs can spiral as well, as rather than waiting for parts to be advertised at the right price, you'll be forced to buy everything new, or from trade suppliers.

You can bet that Jeff Marton has a system in place for his builds, and one that works, too; you'll often find that each successive project becomes easier as you develop your practical and organisational skills.
(Courtesy Jeff Marton)

CHAPTER FOUR

Metal repair & modification

I t's very hard to find a project vehicle these days that has zero rust or previous rust repair work. This chapter covers many of the typical metal repairs that will be needed for different types of air-cooled VW. We'll show the correct way to execute restoration quality repairs, including drilling out factory spot welds and butt-welding techniques. This chapter will also cover some of the popular modifications when lowering a vehicle, such as wheel tubs and chassis notches.

Before we dig deep into how to carry out metal repairs to the various different types of air-cooled

If you're not well-versed in high quality metal repair, it may be worth saving up more money and waiting for a rust free car to come along – they are still out there, albeit harder to find these days. (Courtesy Aastin Bolin)

VW, we should first mention that it is still possible, although rare, to find a car that has zero rust-through and doesn't 'need' any rust repair at all. Cars in many of the southwestern US states, for example, may have been lucky to escape without any rust-through at all; I've seen cars buried in the desert sand that have been lucky enough to escape with original paint still on the areas that were buried, where other cars from the same area have rusted through.

When it comes to finding one of these 'rust free' cars, luck is a major factor, but budget also comes into play, like it or not; the healthier your budget to buy a car in the first place, the better the car you are going to end up with. If you have a high budget and aren't concerned with spending more on buying and restoring a car than what the value of the finished car will be, then more power to you, and you'll likely make life a lot easier for yourself when it comes to the restoration.

Notice how I say 'rust free' in inverted commas? Well, although no two cars ever rust in the same way and you might get lucky and find a Bug with shiny metal inside the heater channels, or a Bus that has zero surface rust or trapped dirt inside the sills/rockers or outriggers, I'd say there is over 90 per cent certainty that these cavity sections will have, at minimum, a very light coat of surface rust, and, at a maximum, packed sand and dirt that is beginning to eat its way through the metal – this is where the phrase rusting from the inside out comes into play.

The thing with 'rust free' desert cars, especially those that sit partially buried in the sand, is that sand has a way of getting inside everything. This is, perhaps, fine when a car is sitting in the desert in the hot summer months, but even the desert gets cold in the winter, and with the cold may come a little damp in the air. When the sand in body cavity sections gets wet, it has a habit of bonding and permanently trapping the moisture against the metal.

If you look at the nice, seasoned coating of surface rust on the top side of a Patina car, then you can guarantee that the same moisture that caused any surface rust to happen has been trapped, for some periods of time, in the inside of the car and the body cavity sections; just look at the inside of the roof of one of these cars when the remains of the headliner are removed and you'll see what I mean. It's harder for moist air to escape from areas like this, so they will rust more heavily as a result.

Dissecting original rust-free body cut sections by drilling out the original factory spot welds – this helps to ensure a factory finish when carrying out repairs. (Author's collection)

When a car remains in this kind of climate, rusting takes a very long time, but as soon as a car arrives in Europe (or other colder, damper climates), the trapped moisture in body cavity sections gets to the point where it is holding dampness against the already surface-rusted metal on a permanent basis – especially if it is either stored outside in the salty winters, or inside a damp garage. If you're hoping to maintain a hardcore Patina car in this kind of climate, whilst attempting to halt the deterioration of such a car, then a Carcoon style bubble, which you park the car inside whilst it circulates dehumidified air permanently inside the bubble, is probably the best option. If you can't stretch to this, then a dehumidifier, along with cavity wax protection and removing floor mats, etc is the next best option.

Getting to cavity areas while you can

The next section may seem ludicrous to some, but it's an important one: if you're looking to restore a car right the first time, especially when it comes to Type 1-3 cars and Karmann Ghias/Type 181s – cars with a separate floorpan – then you'd be wise to drill out the spot welds and remove the heater channel bottom plates – even if they don't look too bad – while you

have the best chance and the body is removed from the floorpan.

As I said, it may seem crazy to some, but it is the only way to eradicate trapped dirt and rust while you have the opportunity to do so. There are perfect new parts available to replace the old ones with, which could be spot welded into position to minimise any welding oxidation. Of course, you could carefully drill out the original factory spot welds to remove the original bottom plates, before cleaning and painting the inside sections, then plug weld the original pieces back into position. The only problems with doing this are that plug welds can cause the paint, which you have just applied to the inside of the area, to burn off and oxidise, which in turn begins to flash rust. Resistance spot welders can be rented and will only burn the paint in a tiny area where the panels are melted together.

Let's face it, removing the body from the floorpan of your car is something you really only want to do once. Restore the car underneath, and be comfortable in the knowledge that it will last another 30-50 years – maybe forever – or at least the car may outlast you, if you store it correctly and keep it clean. Having been around the block a few times and restored/preserved many Patina cars, this is what I would do with any I bought.

Quite often you'll find that you can't drill out spot-welds – here, the only option to effect a factory quality repair is to butt weld together the panels. (Author's collection)

If there's a lot of surface rust on the exterior of the car, such as with Daniel Mandat's vehicle, you can bet that the poorly-painted areas inside the body cavities will also be rusty. (Courtesy Daniel Mandat)

Would I do the same when restoring a Bus – that is, would I chop into body cavity areas, or replace things like outriggers for the sake of doing so when there was no visible rust? No, I wouldn't. I think it's safe to make a distinction between the restoration of separate floorpan cars and those – like the Bus – of unitary construction. The major difference between leaving areas when restoring a Bus that may be trapping inside old dirt and rust is that those areas can be addressed at a later date when the rust eventually begins to eat its way out. Of course, if the Bus is stored correctly from now on, this might never happen.

The other main reason that I wouldn't remove outer body panels on a Bus before it is necessary, is that these panels constitute part of the visible painted body sections, whereas on a separate floorpan car, they are hidden underneath. It's a lot easier to restore these areas, as they can just be given a fresh coat of the body colour paint and no-one will be any the wiser unless they look underneath, at which point they may be fooled into thinking that it's original paint. If you repair or replace sill/rocker panels on a Bus, however, you'll need to match the paint to the surrounding Patina, which is much harder to do correctly.

If the outriggers or jacking points are rusted, or even small sections of the inner sill/rocker, then it's possible to repair or replace these areas without disturbing the outer sill – even if there's the odd bit of surface rust or small rust bubbles – then you'll likely get quite a few more years out of it without needing to replace it. This all depends on how much of a perfectionist you are – Patina cars can take a mindset adjustment, especially if you have fully restored cars in the past.

Even though I have spent my whole adult life in the Patina cars camp, and have never fully restored a car, there are some preservation restorations that I have done, where I'd now do things differently. Remember: a car is only original once – you can always repair it in the future, but you can't un-repair it. As you will see when we come to the paint section, matching Patina effectively brings a lot of factors into play, and many people don't ever come close to doing a good job – one that looks like original paint.

These days, apart from preventative work to areas that are generally unseen or underneath – like heater channel bottom plates and outriggers – I'd choose to leave certain areas alone, even if they have a little

It's important to take a lot of time to get the fit right on repair panels before welding them into position – this can be a very time-consuming process. (Courtesy Craig Yelley/ Vintage VW)

It's not just the body cavities that can suffer: here you see some repairs being carried out on the transmission tunnel on the floorpan of a Type 3 Squareback. (Courtesy Sublime Classic Restorations/Gareth Bayliss-Smith)

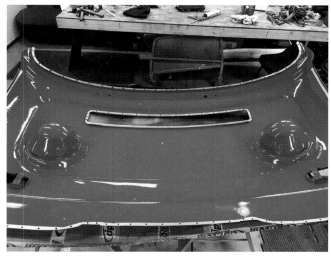

Coating the inside of new panels as best you can gives the repair the best chance of lasting a long time; here, Craig Yelley does a factory quality repair using a Klassicfab nose panel on an early Bay Window Bus. (Courtesy Craig Yelley/Vintage VW)

If you want to do top quality restoration work, then taking the time to do a top quality repair is needed. Not only does a repair like this require a lot of time to line up the panels correctly, but it also takes welding in a series of tacks to allow the heat to dissipate – welding too much in one go will warp the panels. (Courtesy Craig Yelley/Vintage VW)

rust showing. That's really the rule when it comes to preserving originality – until you can no longer turn a blind eye to it: minimum intervention. Choosing to preserve what is there rather than restore is the entire ethos surrounding Patina cars, although both preservation and restoration mean different things to different people; where one person would choose to leave a rusted front bumper on their car, another would feel that this needed to be replaced with a better original one, and a third person may feel that all of the chrome trim should be replaced or re-chromed and that only Patina on the paint is acceptable.

The bottom line is that there are no 'rules' when it comes to restoring cars in a preservation style, you just have to get a feel for what you are prepared to accept and stick to it – other people's opinions are just that – it's your money and your right to restore parts of your car against popular opinion, or to leave parts unrestored that others think should be fixed. People, especially on internet forums and social media, love to give unsolicited advice. Build your car for you and forget what anybody else thinks – if you're unsure and choose to seek advice, then that's different, but social media and forums are usually the worst places to ask for advice unless you want 100 different opinions and heated bickering.

Metal repair – the rules
Having just told you that there are no hard and fast rules when it comes to restoring your car, and having

told you to ignore unsolicited advice, I'm now going to tell you what's not acceptable when it comes to metal repairs. It's your car, of course, but doing any of the following isn't really restoring a car – at best, it's patching it up and making it last a little while longer:

• Welding patches over rust holes
• Gas welding body repairs
• Seam welding body repairs
• Using expanding foam
• Filling holes with body filler or fibreglass

These are the main faux pas when it comes to 'restoring' cars that we've all seen in the past. In countries where there are annual inspection laws, it's likely that these crude repairs may have been carried out in the past in order that the car could pass its annual inspection and, in most cases, it would be simply a case of forming a metal patch or patches to cover a rusted area and then welding/screwing/pop-riveting them over the top of the rusty area. It's not uncommon to find cars with two, three, or four patches over the original rust holes, which all need to be removed before a correct repair can be done.

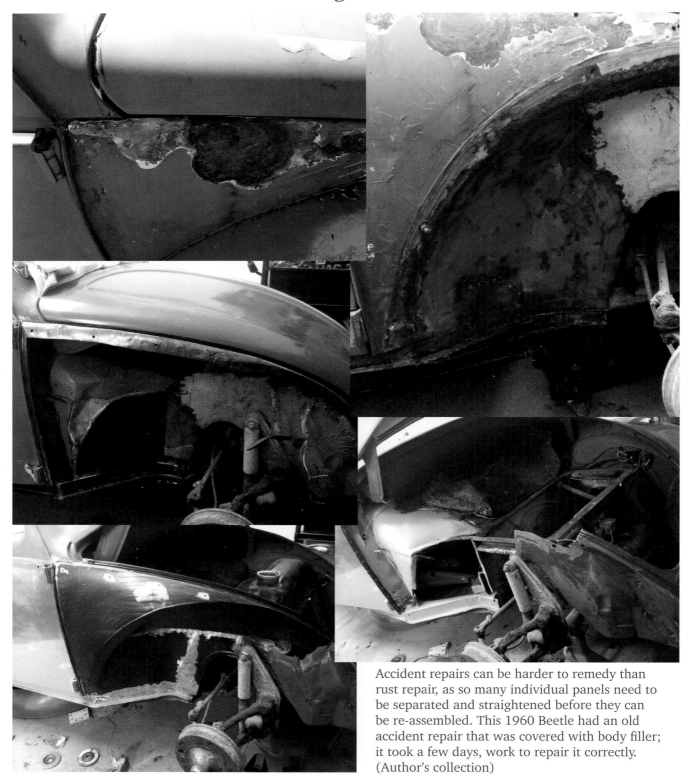

Accident repairs can be harder to remedy than rust repair, as so many individual panels need to be separated and straightened before they can be re-assembled. This 1960 Beetle had an old accident repair that was covered with body filler; it took a few days, work to repair it correctly. (Author's collection)

Get some skills

Let's start by saying that no-one is born with metalworking skills – they have to be learned. How you choose to learn is up to you: take courses, observe and learn with a friend, or practice on scrap sheet metal until you become proficient enough to do a

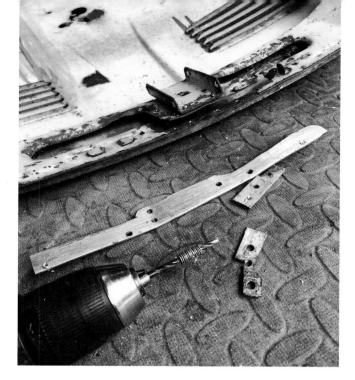

Pop-riveting panels in position is a sure-fire bodge – it would have taken less time to repair the area properly with a welder. (Author's collection)

This machine will likely come with a gas regulator for small, disposable gas bottles – this is not economical, and isn't anywhere near as good as getting a proper regulator and larger refillable bottles, even if you have to sign up to a contract with a gas supplier. When it comes to choosing gas, Argon burns hotter than CO2, but has other danger implications and is deadly if inhaled – careful storage is a major issue here. I've found that Argon/CO2 mix gas is the best all-rounder for car body repairs and thicker sheet metal on chassis areas; it also produces a better quality weld.

decent job. If you can't be bothered to learn these skills or invest in the right tools and equipment, then just save up and pay someone with a good reputation for high-quality metalwork, and insist on progress pictures of each repair.

When it comes to getting qualified to tackle repairs, the best place to start would be night classes in MIG welding. This will likely teach you how to weld thicker steel than you would normally be welding with car repairs, but at least it will show you how to set up the machine correctly and show you the pitfalls of MIG welding. Setting up the machine is possibly the hardest part of MIG welding, and the one thing that many get wrong. A course will get you to recognise the 'sizzling bacon' sound of a good weld and how to differentiate this from the sound of a porous weld.

MIG vs flux core/gasless MIG
Following on from getting some skills, by far the best possible investment you can make is to invest in a good quality MIG welder, and avoid cheaper gasless MIG or flux core machines. When it comes down to it, these gasless options are a cheap option for people who just want to join two pieces of metal together. If you're serious about making a good job of your car – and others in the future – then dig deep and buy the best machine you can buy. Avoid anything less than around 130A when it comes to buying a MIG welder, as they aren't man enough to do any thicker steel repairs and also will get too hot if used for an extended period of time.

Buy the best quality repair panels you can for the job. Using sub-standard panels will always result in a sub-par result. This rear bumper mount from Hooky's panel shop is great. (Author's collection)

Setting up/storing your machine
When it comes to setting up your welder, 0.8mm wire will produce a better weld than 0.6mm wire, so you'll need to upgrade the wire and the tip. It's also worth seeing what upgrades are available in terms of the actual welding torch for the machine you buy – a professional torch will be much easier to use than the flimsy 'hobby' torch that is standard on most low-to-moderate priced welders. Price is obviously a factor when it comes to buying a welder, but try to buy based on good reviews and avoid really cheap or unproven brands if you can. If you're tempted to buy a better quality used machine, then this can be a good idea, but

Sectioning-in panels is the best way to go about repairing a car without losing too much of the original metal. Large panels like this will warp even worse if you concentrate the heat too much from welding; go slowly, moving around the panel with one tack at a time and allow plenty of cooling time as you go.
(Courtesy Craig Yelley/Vintage VW)

check where it was stored, as poor storage results in oxidation/rust on the welding wire and other internal components. If buying used, then you should be able to demo the machine.

Drilling out spot welds

One of the best skills you can learn when attempting factory-quality repairs on these cars is locating and drilling out factory spot welds. Replacing panels in this way means you're effectively making the car as good as when it left the factory – this is the preferred way of repairing or replacing smaller panels, or panels that are too far gone to replace. Finding spot welds in areas with heavy rust, old glue, or under old seam sealer can be a challenge. Having the area blasted, or going over with a wire wheel on a grinder can help to locate them, but sometimes even this will not make the welds easy to see; in this case, try running your finger over the area to feel for dimples. If you find it easier,

Breaking free the remnants of an original panel after drilling out the factory spot welds.
(Author's collection)

Filling large holes with seam sealer, expanding foam, newspaper, chicken wire, or body filler is not a restoration quality repair! (Author's collection)

Plug welding vs spot welding

Once you've removed the old spot welds and taken out the rusted panel/piece, clean and de-rust the area, and paint it with a zinc-rich weld-through primer before fitting the new panel. When it comes to how you'll weld on the new piece, spot welding is how it was done at the factory, and is technically superior for a variety of reasons. Spot welding only produces very localised heat, and will not burn off paint or cause oxidation on the back of the repaired area. Spot welding also creates the dimples on the panel, replicating factory repairs. Spot welders are expensive to buy though (look for tool rental in your area), and sometimes the jaws aren't deep enough to be used on larger panels.

Plug welding is similar to spot welding, in that it's effectively joining panels in the same way as spot welding. Plug welding requires you to drill holes in the repair panel – usually a minimum of 6mm – which you can weld through to join the two panels. If you're plug welding, then investing in an air-powered hole punch will be quicker and produce much neater holes than drilling. If you are

you could put a dot with a Sharpie pen where you locate the centre of the spot weld.

Spot weld drill bits can be bought reasonably cheaply – they are available in 6mm and 8mm and I've had success with both. 8mm tends to cut out the whole of the weld, but they take longer to cut through and tend to go blunt quicker. Drilling out spot welds should be done on low speed, stopping regularly to check your progress. Quite often, you'll know when you've broken the weld, as you'll see a small puff of rusty dust come out of the weld. Trying to separate the panels with a sharp cold chisel will show you if you have drilled far enough. As you drill subsequent welds, it can help to separate the layers – this will also help you to see any spot welds that you missed. If you cut through too far – all the way through the next panel – then that's not ideal, and you'll have to weld up this hole before fitting the new panel. It happens to all of us at some point, though.

Sectioning-in cab floor corners on a Bus requires a mixture of plug/spot welding and butt welding techniques in order to make a factory looking repair.
(Courtesy Craig Yelley/Vintage VW)

The only way to properly replace floorpan halves is to split the body from the 'pan – this way you can get to both sides with ease, and metal finish the repairs. (Courtesy Sublime Classic Restorations/Gareth Bayliss-Smith)

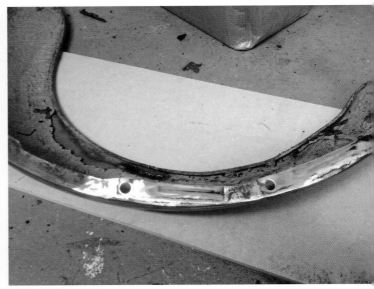

Wing/fender mounting flanges often need fresh metal 'letting in,' as moisture and road dirt/salt creeps in between. (Author's collection)

drilling, drill over a solid wood block with minimal pressure and clean up the back of the drilled hole with a flap disc before proceeding with the fitting and welding.

The correct technique for plug welding is to securely hold the metal together with a clamp on each side of the hole you are about to weld, and aim the welding wire at the centre of the hole, ie the panel you're welding to. As you weld, build up a small pool of weld by gently swirling the torch. Aim for moderate power and short duration to minimise heat build-up. With some practice, you should be able to get nice flat plug welds that need minimal grinding – adjust the wire speed as you go to get the optimal weld. Rather than welding in a row, move the clamps to another area, and take steps to minimise too much heat build-up in one area.

Butt welding

In areas where you're going to make a repair in the middle of a panel, you'll need to butt weld the join.

In reality, many repairs are a mixture of spot or plug welding and butt welding. Some people prefer to lap weld joints, putting in a joggled or stepped edge before lapping one panel over the top of another. These people argue that lap welding in this manner is stronger, but in reality, it creates a moisture trap, especially as the lapped joint isn't continuously welded, and will eventually allow moisture to creep into the joint.

The beauty of butt welding, if done correctly, is that, in many cases, you can metal finish it both inside and out, making it no different than it would have been originally, as a whole panel. We're not going to cover lap welding here, as, in my opinion, it isn't really a restoration quality repair. Butt welding can take a lot of practice to get right, and takes a lot of patience to get a good result. The main difficulty when it comes to butt welding, is warpage – it's very easy to warp the panels with too much heat, or when not leaving a gap for the welding wire to fill – many people assume that the panels have to be touching, but this isn't the case.

When planning to successfully butt weld a panel, the largest portion of time is spent in the fitting stage. The amount of time you take to make sure you have an even gap around the repair and that the panels are securely clamped in position, will equate to how good the finished repair is. The panels need to be completely flat – held at exactly the same level, in order to prevent you blowing holes and warp the repair. The gap needs to be the same as the thickness of the welding wire. If you do find the gap has narrowed once you've placed

What happens on the back of a panel when you weld the front: oxidation and paint blistering occurs, which will eventually turn to rust if untreated. This is especially problematic on cavity sections. (Author's collection)

Sometimes, as in the case of this Split Bus roof peak, a section will have to be cut out, straightened, and welded back into position. This dent was so bad before that it had also deflected the lower lip upward. (Author's collection)

a tack on the area, planishing the tack weld with a planishing hammer will open up the gap again.

I'll leave the pictures and captions to illustrate the rest of both techniques – at the end of the day, getting your hands dirty and practising each type of joint on scrap metal is more beneficial than listening to a wordy description. The pictures will help to guide you and show you how things should look, but there's no substitute for practice and experience. If you've always put off learning to weld or thought you can't do it, actually learning how – and realising that it's not as difficult as you expected – will be a very rewarding experience. Perhaps most rewarding of all is that you'll view new project cars in a different light, knowing that you can fix them yourself.

If you take your time butt welding in repair panels, you should be able to metal finish the repair; a 40-grit flap disc on an angle grinder was carefully used to grind back the weld until almost invisible. (Author's collection)

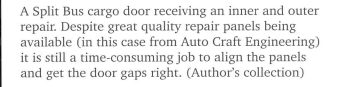

A Split Bus cargo door receiving an inner and outer repair. Despite great quality repair panels being available (in this case from Auto Craft Engineering) it is still a time-consuming job to align the panels and get the door gaps right. (Author's collection)

Johnny Montana removes a section of a pattern heater channel to make it look more factory; better quality parts have become available in the past few years from BBT, Klassicfab and others. (Author's collection)

Removing a rusted cab floor section by drilling out the spot-welds and splitting them with a cold chisel.
(Author's collection)

Repairing a lower nose panel on a Split Bus; a common 'repair' in the USA was to drill a series of holes and pull out dents. Nowadays, a stud welder and slide hammer would achieve similar results but without the holes and extra distortion. (Author's collection)

CHAPTER FIVE
Paint finishes & how to achieve them

Recreating Patina to match the rest of the paint finish on a Patina car is a very complex and difficult thing to achieve correctly. This chapter explores the different techniques you can employ for different types of Patina, from mild paint fade to heavily rusted panels.

When it comes to recreating Patina on an area of a car that has been repaired, no two cars are ever the same. Many people assume that doing a Patina paint job on a car is a simple matter of painting it as you

Many people assume that genuine Patina, such as that on Nate Jones' car, can be re-created by sanding paint and allowing it to rust. This couldn't be further from the truth. (Author's collection)

would with a normal restoration, then sanding through the new paint to reveal as much primer as possible and possibly also some bare metal, which will then rust. This kind of treatment, however, will only ever result in a fake Patina look.

As I've said in previous chapters, no two cars will ever rust the same or fade the same – factors such as what angle a car was parked in relation to the sun, what colour the car was originally (darker colours absorb more heat and fade more), and whether a car was repainted at some point – all add to how a car will look after 30+ years baking in the midday sun and being exposed to whatever humidity there was where the car was resting.

Observe other cars of the same type
Being successful at 'faking it' – Patina paint blending – is as much about how much you observe and pay attention than the actual skills themselves. How many people, for example, when they are paint blending a body panel, spend hours looking at the same panel on similar vehicles online to see just how the equivalent vehicle would 'typically' rust? As I've said, each and every car fades differently, but there are typical areas that fade more than others on Patina cars.

Take Split Buses for example: if you look at the front nose panel of a Split Bus with moderate to heavy Patina, you'll see that the areas above the headlights have a bulge that picks up a lot of heat from the sun – the lower nose panel may otherwise have strong original paint, but it's likely that, even on a mild Patina Bus, this upper headlight area will have begun to get sunburn. To re-create Patina in this area will require

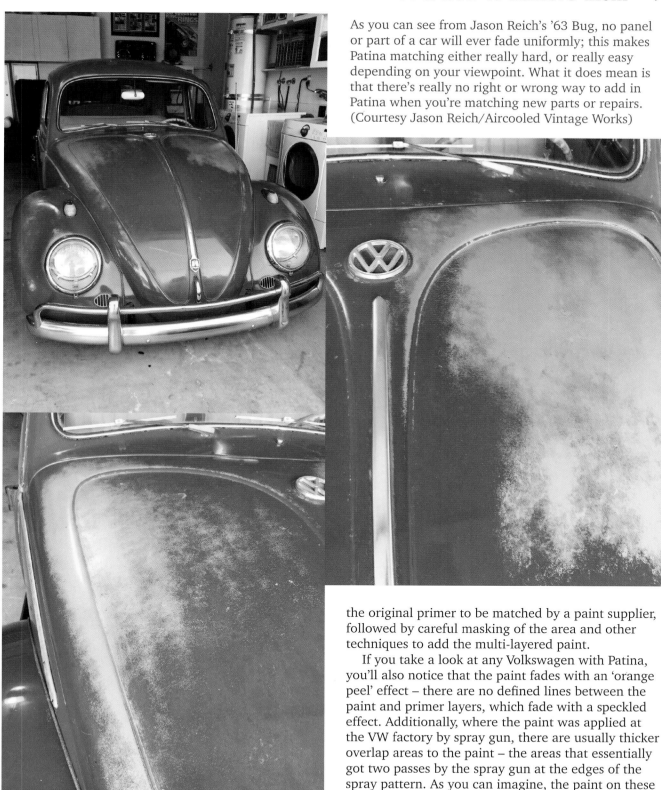

As you can see from Jason Reich's '63 Bug, no panel or part of a car will ever fade uniformly; this makes Patina matching either really hard, or really easy depending on your viewpoint. What it does mean is that there's really no right or wrong way to add in Patina when you're matching new parts or repairs. (Courtesy Jason Reich/Aircooled Vintage Works)

the original primer to be matched by a paint supplier, followed by careful masking of the area and other techniques to add the multi-layered paint.

If you take a look at any Volkswagen with Patina, you'll also notice that the paint fades with an 'orange peel' effect – there are no defined lines between the paint and primer layers, which fade with a speckled effect. Additionally, where the paint was applied at the VW factory by spray gun, there are usually thicker overlap areas to the paint – the areas that essentially got two passes by the spray gun at the edges of the spray pattern. As you can imagine, the paint on these areas is twice as thick as the rest of the paint, so when it is exposed to the sun for many years, these overlap areas are the last to be burned off. This results in

Mark Fulton from T2D built this awesome hardcore Patina Bug; it was given a full body-off restoration underneath and a custom interior. Studying the Patina in detail on cars like this can really help when it comes to re-creating Patina on repaired areas. (Courtesy Mark Fulton)

My Pearl White '66 Walkthru Bus had a killer fade on the nose panel; this was after removing all the rust staining with some limescale remover and a green scourer. Note how one side is faded more than the other. (Author's collection)

horizontal or vertical stripes, depending on how they applied the paint at the factory.

Lower colour first

When it comes to two-tone Buses, Volkswagen always painted the lower colour first over the whole Bus, before masking up and applying the upper colour. This results in tremendous Patina paint, as the upper layer

Note the 'orange peel' like fade on the areas of this Bus where the paint remains. Most people think that there's a defined line where the paint stops and the primer starts, but this is rarely ever the case. Note also the two different primer colours. (Author's collection)

Different paint colours react in different ways to the heat of the sun. Karl Fennell's Mango Green/Seagull Grey Bus has little to no fade at the front and much more on the passenger side than the driver side. This points to this side and rear corner being positioned where most of the sun's heat was for a few years. Had this been a darker colour, such as Titian Red, it would likely have lost a lot more paint. (Courtesy Karl Fennell)

of paint is usually the first to go – it's closer to the sun after all – it's not uncommon to see two-tone Buses that have none of the upper half colour on them, due to years of baking in the sun. If you're looking to faithfully re-create Patina on the upper half of such a Bus, you'll need to apply the correct coloured primer layers, followed by the lower half colour, then the upper half colour.

Moving back to the example of a correct Patina fade on a Split Bus, when it comes to the upper nose area on a two-tone Bus, you'll see that the area underneath the windscreen surround bears the brunt of the sun exposure, with the heaviest fading at the top, after which it can gradually fade to thick original paint. This all depends on the rest of the Bus – maybe it sat for 40 years with one side facing the main midday heat of the sun. This can result in vehicles that have virtually no perceptible Patina on one side, and literally no paint on the other.

As you give your project the initial clean and appraisal, you'll likely wash off some of the milky layers of dead paint, exposing more Patina in the process. Take good before and after pictures of the washing process, so you can see if there's any extra fading – you'll be able to carefully study these pictures on your computer to see a pattern of

You can clearly see that Volkswagen painted two-tone Buses in the lower colour first, followed by the upper colour on Michael Schramm's Sea Blue/Cumulus White 13-window Deluxe. (Courtesy Michael Schramm)

fading so you can sympathetically add in paint to the areas that need it, without it standing out a mile.

As you re-apply paint to your project, there may be some areas where there is no Patina at all in the finish and the paint looks factory fresh. Don't be tempted to try to Patinate these areas as you paint them; if they have strong surrounding original paint and you try to add Patina, it'll stand out a mile, look fake, and ruin the finished product. Remember that you're looking to sympathetically match what was there (or would have been there in the case of a missing panel) without going overboard.

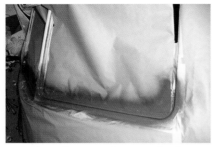

Painting the Sea Blue on the lower windscreen surround of my '66 Bus prior to painting the white – this is so the correct colour is underneath if the upper paint were to fade in the future. (Author's collection)

You can clearly see that the upper portion of the nose panel on my old Mouse Grey '63 Bus has faded first, but there is still a lot of strong paint elsewhere, despite the Bus being in a New Mexico junkyard for 40 years. (Author's collection)

Factory 'reject' panels

A hot topic of debate on the forums at www.thesamba.com a few years ago was the use of panels fitted at the factory, which, when the top layer of paint was burned off by the sun, exposed a different factory colour underneath. I say a hot topic because some people couldn't be convinced that these panels weren't replaced later after accident damage, despite several people owning cars with a similar look – many of these were one-owner cars that had never been in an accident.

Crucially, all of the cars supporting the theory that these panels were fitted by Volkswagen itself, all had a paint colour from the correct model year underneath the colour which had begun to burn off. The theory behind Volkswagen repainting and fitting these panels holds a lot of weight, as Volkswagen was very fastidious about its quality control process back in the day – this was even the subject of many of the original Doyle Dane Bernbach VW adverts.

It only makes sense that if a body panel was rejected at the quality control process, removed, and replaced with another new body panel, that the 'reject' panel would go back through the painting process to be re-used on another car further down the production line. If you buy a project car that has this multi-toned paint finish, don't be too quick to try and cover it up with new paint, or attempt to eradicate the extra (wrong) colour – it's very likely that this panel was repainted at the VW factory and refitted to your car during the production process. Volkswagen couldn't predict that these cars would last 50 plus years, and that the new paint would be burned off by the sun.

When it comes to cars that have a covering of surface rust on them, many people don't realise that there is usually primer still left on the car underneath the surface rust staining – usually around 80% of what you see when you look at rusted metal is the staining from rust getting damp. Tony Wysinger was one of the first guys I know to show how easy it was to clean off this rust staining to expose original primer underneath – Tony uses a product called CLR (Calcium, Lime, Rust) on his cars, combined with a kitchen green scourer to remove heavy rust staining.

When you really think about it, the fact that primer is left underneath the rust staining makes sense – primer is porous, so when the topcoat is burned off and the primer is exposed, the moisture is then allowed to seep in through the primer to the metal. Ironically, especially in dry climates, the resulting covering of rust staining acts like a protective layer, stopping the hot sun from burning the primer off. Many people love the hardcore Patina look of rust staining, but just as many prefer the polished Patina

One of the rear wings on James Peene's 1966 Beetle was Java Green under the Ruby Red; it's very possible that this wing was pulled by a quality control checker from the production line and repainted red. (Courtesy James Peene)

It would be hard to tell if the Indigo Blue decklid in Jeff Marton's car was a result of production line quality control, but testing some thinners on a small spot would prove it either way: thinners won't remove factory paint. (Courtesy Jeff Marton)

It's likely that the Clementine bonnet/hood was repainted Elm Green in the factory production process on this 1970 Beetle. (Author's collection)

Steve Parsons could have removed the rust staining on his '60 Kombi with a product like CLR, but chose to leave it with the as-found survivor look. (Courtesy Joss Ashley)

If you want to know the difference that CLR or other limescale and rust removal products can make, here's an example on a Chevy wing by Tony Wysinger, who made the use of CLR popular on VW forums in the USA. (Courtesy Tony Wysinger)

Although Sloan Bush's '65 Pearl White Microbus had a lot of strong original paint, this picture illustrates how rust staining can be removed with CLR or other limescale removal products. (Courtesy Sloan Bush)

look of original primer with some visible darker rust – the choice is yours, but you need to make the choice before you start to remove any rust staining or scrub anything too hard.

So, as you're beginning to see, re-creating Patina paint is actually a very involved process. When you read the above, it makes you realise that Patina cars aren't an easy option and the owners aren't 'lazy,' as some opinionated folks would say. Owning and sympathetically restoring a Patina car is actually an art form and a painstaking process. On top of everything listed above, when it comes to Patina cars, there are lots of choices when it comes to the type of finish you want on the project. As mentioned in more detail in Chapter 1, the type of Patina finish you prefer for the car can be dictated by the car itself, but you still have a lot of choices for which route you go down.

To buff or not to buff

The first decision you'll need to make is whether to buff the paint, or whether to leave it dull. Some people have a distinct preference for one particular look, whereas others build different cars in different ways. Some cars do lend themselves to an original dull finish – I often think Split Beetles simply look better when the paint is left dull, like PJ Gibbons' car, or Drew Pritchard's '52 Sunroof.

Rich Rivera's '58 Ragtop Bug had a fair bit more original paint left on it than this when first purchased; buffing the car removed a lot of the dead paint to leave a lot of factory primer on show. (Courtesy Richard Rivera)

Chadd Magee recommissioned this Turkis '62 'Terry the Turk' for his partner, Kat; buffing the paint was part of the recipe. (Courtesy Chadd Magee)

As you can see on Chase Hill's old Beetle, the lower panels of the car barely had much Patina in comparison with the upper portion of the car; not all blended/replaced panels need to be Patinated, to do so would be overkill on many cars. (Courtesy Chase Hill)

As someone who has always had a preference for buffing original paint and rocking the 'polished Patina' look, I'm now coming around to the duller 'as discovered' look on certain cars. This dulled look paints a picture, or tells a story of an old car that has been left to its own devices – maybe it's a barn find, or maybe it's been sat in a field for 30 years, but the paint finish tells a story – like the analogy of an old French house with peeling paint on the shutters that I've used before.

For many people, the dull paint of the car, or the peeling paint on the shutters of the house, is the entire reason that they were attracted to it in the first place. Although the natural tendency of people is to want to restore, or 'improve' things, the unfortunate and often unseen consequence is that the car (or house) loses the appeal that it had when it was a project with untold potential.

Paint matching

Having said all of this, I'll go on the record and say that getting paint matched to polished paint is much easier than trying to match dulled paint, both in colour and finish. What's more, if you do decide to keep a car in a dull finish and have paint mixed to suit this, the paint will only match the car until someone decides they want to polish the car – no amount of wet sanding and polishing will bring a shine to paint that has had a matting agent mixed into it – so these areas will need

This Sealing Wax Red/Beige Grey survivor has polished paint; this makes people realise that it's loved and cherished, rather than appearing like a neglected vehicle that needs paint. (Courtesy @10ft_Doug)

to be repainted again if you (or a subsequent owner) decides to polish the car.

I'd actually advise that you get paint mixed in gloss, rather than have a matting agent applied – you can then dull the paint with fine wire wool, a Scotch-Brite pad or 600-1000 grit wet and dry paper. Getting a good paint match on a dull paint finish takes a very patient paint mixer – as with glossy paint, you really

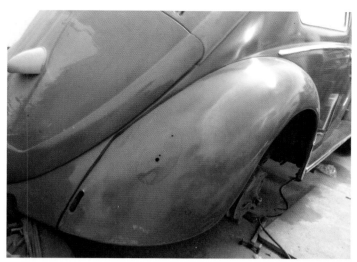

If you don't get a good paint match, including the layers of paint or primer under the topcoat, the whole paint blend just won't work – the paint match is the most important part. (Author's collection)

Figuring out a match to all of the individual different paint finish elements on a Bus like Jerry Lemieux's 'Burnt Westy' is a really involved process. (Courtesy Shin Watanabe)

need to dry the mixed paint as fully as possible, as the colour will usually change as it dries. I've lost count of the times I've had paint mixed which looks like a perfect match when wet, only to go a few shades darker when it cures. By this time, the only option is to go back to the paint supplier for another match to be done, and to sand down the car and start again. This gets really tedious, really fast. It doesn't matter what other techniques you use to age paint, if the paint match is wrong it won't look right whatever you do.,

It doesn't help that most auto paint suppliers just don't 'get' Patina. They have literally no understanding of what you are trying to achieve and also look at you as if you're crazy. They've spent a lifetime mixing paint for people who are trying to 'fix' cars – to make them perfect – and then you come along and want them to help you maintain the imperfect. This is a completely new area that many paint shops have never paid any mind to, so you can appreciate that it takes a lot of mental adjustment: many shops just aren't prepared to take the time to accommodate your needs in this respect.

In a sense, you'd probably be better trying to get an antique restorer to match the paint for you, or, better still, leave the paint matching to a professional – if you can find one. When it comes to auto paint suppliers, you really want to find a company with an 'old boy' who mixes the paint – these older guys usually have a lot of knowledge that's hard to pass down to successive generations. Their job is also being made much harder now that certain chemicals and lead have been outlawed in the colour toners that were traditionally used. Now that cellulose paint has been outlawed and single stage paint is all water-based, many of the toners just can't replicate original cellulose colours; you'll have to make sure that they get the paint match in natural light – if it's done under artificial light, it won't match once you wheel your painted car outside.

Before going to any old paint supplier to get paint matched, ask around on social media, internet forums, or at car shows. Don't be afraid to approach people with Patina cars and ask them about the paint – if they've done any repairs and who did them, who matched the paint, etc. I'd say it is far

If you try to get the paint mixed to the original VW paint code on a car like Cody Goss' Ruby Red '61, it will likely be way off: paint mixed to a code should only be used for underside repairs. (Courtesy Cody Goss)

When attempting to convincingly blend paint onto a car like Nick Bevis' Turkis Bug, you'll need to match the paint to several different areas and carefully mask up large areas when adding paint. (Courtesy Andrew Thompson/AThompsonsPhoto)

etter to put in the leg work in advance, and even to use a paint supplier who is far away from where you live if other people have used them and can offer a recommendation. Speaking from experience, if the colour match is wrong, it will stand out a mile and no matter what you try to do to match any Patina, it just won't work.

When it comes to getting paint mixed, the only time that you should ever get paint mixed to the original paint code is when you're painting underneath parts of

Volkswagen used different primer colours on different coloured cars, as well as two different coloured primer layers – matching both primer colours as well as the topcoat will result in a much better finish. (Courtesy @10ft_Doug)

the car – heater channel bottoms, inner wings, etc. These are areas that haven't been exposed to the sun and won't have faded. Even interior parts are exposed to the sun and will have faded to a degree. When getting the paint matched for other areas, there is no substitute for getting a match to an original body panel.

The caveat to the above statement is the fact that your car won't have faded evenly all over – certain areas of the car will have faded more, so if you get the paint matched to the front of the car, then it may not match the rear so well. Did I mention yet that Patina matching is pretty hard?!

Different primer colours for different colours

When getting primer matched for Patina paint blending, I usually get it matched in gloss, not primer – the gloss is not porous like the original primer and will last longer. Original VW primers also polish to a high gloss, so the gloss primer won't look out of place once it is on the car. Don't just assume that leftover paint that you have already had matched to the primer on another car will match the primer on the car you're now working on – VW used different primer tones for certain colours – lighter colours often had a lighter primer and high pigment colours that have a great degree of transparency, such as yellows

or oranges, will almost certainly have a white primer layer.

You'll notice when studying pictures of Patina cars, that there are usually at least two different primer layers – a light to medium grey on top of a darker grey. If your car is a hardcore Patina car, with a lot of fade going on, then it's likely you'll have to match both primer colours and the topcoat colour.

Convincing paint to primer fade

As well as studying the areas where Patina would typically happen on a car of your model type and colour, take some time to study the pattern of Patina fade on similar cars too – you can replicate this with careful masking of the primer areas before you apply the topcoats – liquid masking solution can work better than tape, as it dries as latex and can be rubbed off after use. If you have a large amount of primer showing, figure out a shape of the primer patch that looks similar to the surrounding paintwork. Once you've done this, you can mask off a large and unevenly shaped patch, using soft tape lines – fold back the masking tape on itself, so that there isn't a defined line – this stops the paint from forming a ridge at the edge of the patch.

Once you've masked off the patch, you can blow on the paint with an aerosol can – use light strokes when getting near the masked area, so that the

Some cars, like Randy Slack's amazing Oval dash Karmann Kab, have very defined areas of primer fade; to match paint on a car like this it would be necessary to paint large areas in the primer colour alone, without any of the original paint colour needing to be added, except as orange peel effect to fade between areas – there's never a defined line between paint and primer. (Courtesy Andrew Thompson/AThompsonsPhoto)

You can clearly see the orange peel graduation between paint, primer, and rust staining in this picture of Nick Bevis' car. In order to achieve convincing paint repairs you'll need to use one of the methods described here to add this orange peel stippling back in. (Courtesy Andrew Thompson/ AThompsonsPhoto)

On Jeff Marton's Sealing Wax Red Single Cab you can see that there's some black paint that has been added at some point and nearly completely faded off; this just adds to the rich tapestry that is Mother Nature's work at its best. Faking a paint finish like this takes the work of a very patient artist. (Courtesy Jeff Marton)

paint is thinner in this area. Once you've built up a couple of coats, you can peel off the masking tape and allow the paint to dry. With a few hours drying time, you're ready to move to the next step – blending in the edges so that it looks like convincing original Patina. Before you can apply any other paint effects to fade in the edges, feel the masked lines with your fingers – if there is a ridge, it'll need to be gently wet sanded off with 600-1000 wet and dry before you proceed.

Paint effects to blend in

When it comes to blending in Patina patches to original paint, there would never be a solid line on an area of original paint with Patina – the paint initially fades like orange peel – stippled areas of paint dots are usually the last parts of the original paint to disappear once it fades through to the primer. There are several ways you can replicate this and it's up to you to find which technique from the following will work in your own application.

1. Speckling paint with an aerosol can or airbrush

It's possible to speckle on paint with an aerosol can by pressing the nozzle very lightly – the paint will speckle onto the panel in blobs of various sizes. I've used this to great effect in the past when matching the Patina on a Sea Blue Split Bus door – the original door was missing and I had to match a white door to the Bus. This technique can be a bit hit and miss, but if you practice the technique on a scrap panel, it can

My 1966 Sea Blue Bus: the texture on the door was added by speckling paint on with an aerosol can, but ultimately the colour match was too dark, so it was sanded down and redone. (Author's collection)

Second go at the paint match was much better – it's hard to tell that this was originally a white driver's door. (Author's collection)

Viewing the (now polished) door from a distance, it would be hard to tell that this wasn't original paint. The work has to stand up to scrutiny both close-up and from further away. (Author's collection)

provide great results. Sometimes with this technique, it's necessary to wet sand the area after the paint has dried, in order to flatten the paint blobs out.

2. Blow painting – spray diffuser

An old school blow painting setup like you may have used in Art class at school can provide similar results to above, although it's usually more controllable – you can get spray diffusers that will hold a small amount of paint and count on either lung power or an air bulb on the end to spray paint out. Similar to the aerosol method above, you'll have to wet sand it once dried to flatten out the surface.

3. Dabbing with a towel or natural sponge

Another way to get a stippled paint effect onto a panel to fade from paint to primer, is to spray paint onto an old towel or natural sponge with an aerosol can and dab this onto the area – this can be one of the most useful methods to get the trademark orange peel fading look that Patina VWs always have. As with all of these methods, it may take some time experimenting to get just the look that you want – experiment on a scrap panel first, before letting yourself loose on your car.

4. Using a small paintbrush

Although it will potentially be a lot more time-consuming, using several different sizes of small artist's paintbrushes to dab individual blobs onto the area is much more controllable than using any of the above methods – this could particularly be used after one of the above techniques, to add in some 'freckles' in some areas, without overdoing it. This method can also be used to add 'rust', by using several different colours on the orange to brown spectrum. You can even dip the end of the handle in the paint for smaller speckles.

Matching rust

Similar to adding dots and orange peel as above, matching rust can be done by using a variety of oranges to browns in matt finish paint to dot rust onto a panel; this is a method many people in the antique world use to match Patina on items, without causing actual rust. Sure, you could use one of a number of products to add proper rust – vinegar, salt, lemon juice, phosphoric acid, etc, but the problem with this (and even with the paint that contains iron filings) is that they can eventually rust or ruin the panel they are applied to. Also, the rust that will form will be fresh rust – this has a bright orange colour, whereas older, more seasoned rust contains darker browns.

Using enamel/craft paints will make it easier to mix and will be more resistant to chemicals when it dries. The beauty of using enamel paints is that any mistakes can be removed with reducer, which will not affect cellulose/water-based aerosol paints. This means it's easy to experiment and wipe off mistakes.

It goes without saying that this kind of work is very time-consuming to get right and can take days of work, even on a small panel or area. The key, as with any of the Patination techniques listed, is to do less, rather than more – it's very tempting to keep on adding more and more colours and areas on a panel, before realising that you've overdone it.

A good tactic to use when doing any kind of Patina work is to do a small amount, then leave it and go back another day – take a picture at the end of each session and study it against other Patina cars to see if and where your work could be improved. Don't forget, perfection is the enemy of done – you'd be surprised how convincing your work will look to most people, even if you're not 100% happy with it.

Steve Parsons begins to add 'rust' to the Salvage Hunters car with a paintbrush; around 80 per cent of the bonnet of this car had to be repainted due to being dented and the rust creeping under the factory etch primer. (Author's collection)

Although this door already had significant Patina, there was a dent that had been repaired with body filler which needed to be rectified before the paint could be blown in. After this, Steve matches the Patina on the repainted parts of the door. (Author's collection)

The door after the work had been carried out: letting in new paint but leaving the old Patina was the tricky part. (Author's collection)

It's hard to believe that the decklid, rear valance and rear wings of this car needed significant amounts of new paint; the decklid paint was entirely new, but with a few paint effects from Steve it appears to be original Patina. (Author's collection)

This entire wing was a different colour when the car was stripped back to original paint; Steve added in some fake Patina to match that on the rest of the car. You can see that he even matched the usual rust runs down from the headlamp screw. (Author's collection)

It's important to keep taking a step back when doing this kind of work, and to limit the tendency to overdo it and add too much paint. (Author's collection)

The finished result as a whole looks like a genuine Patina car, despite the fact that large parts of the car needed paint. (Author's collection)

Close-up of one of the front wings shows how convincing the work can be, especially with the added texture from the different layers of enamel paint and the cardboard pallet. (Author's collection)

Stripping off repainted layers

As I mentioned earlier in the book, repainted layers with a Patina all their own can look amazing and unique in their own right. If you do decide to strip repainted layers off a car though, you'll need to realise that it may take 100 hours to do it right – if you can't afford this kind of time commitment, then it may be better to leave it as is, or sell the car and look for another project. If you do begin the stripping process, you will also likely go through a fair few different products and techniques and spend a pretty penny on different chemicals and consumables.

Paint stripping – least aggressive first

There have been so many different types of paint products on the market over the years, that you won't know how big the task ahead of you is until you begin. The best approach to take is to start with the least aggressive methods first and progress slowly.

1. Paint thinner/acetone

The first product to try is paint thinner or acetone; you'll need chemical resistant gloves for this, as it's nasty stuff and will eat through latex or nitrile gloves in short order. Apply with a cloth initially and rub to see if any paint is coming off on the cloth. If the cloth doesn't seem to be working properly, try some #0000 steel wool (fine) and work in a circular motion in one small spot. If this is working, rinse regularly and change to a new spot on the steel wool. As soon as you see original paint, switch to a cloth again and try to wipe the remainder off. If you find that the cloths clog up too quickly, then try applying the thinners with a paintbrush, which can be easier to work into the paint. You can then wipe off with a cloth.

2. Oven cleaner

As above, test the oven cleaner on a small spot first and leave for 20 seconds, before wiping off. Gradually increase the time you leave the oven cleaner on the panel until you're at 15-20 minutes – if it hasn't worked in this time, then it's unlikely to work at all. Try to work it with steel wool after a while to see if this helps.

Believe it or not, this is the same car as the one in the above pictures; when purchased it was matt black with an orange layer and white layer underneath that. I was tasked with the job of stripping the car back to original paint and carrying out some sympathetic Patina blending for an episode of the *Salvage Hunters: Classic Cars* TV show. (Author's collection)

Unfortunately, when the car was purchased, someone had begun to strip the repainted layers with a combination of oven cleaner and sanding. Had they tried thinners first, they would have realised that the paint could be removed with less abrasive methods, which would damage the original paint less. (Author's collection)

On the first filming day for the car, I tried a few small areas with thinners and a rag; after a small amount of effort, all three layers wiped off, exposing the original paint. (Author's collection)

3. Graffiti remover

Graffiti remover is another product used a lot to strip repainted cars. As above, test a small spot and gradually build up the duration, also trying steel wool to help with paint removal. Some types of paint will respond in seconds, where others will take a lot longer.

4. Wet sanding

Once you've tried the above, or if you're getting down through the layers and can see a little of the original paint colour, switch to wet sanding with 1200 wet and dry paper – use the paper wet with

You can clearly see all three repaint layers on this door, as well as the patch of bondo covering a small dent. The oven cleaner and sanding that had been carried out prior to me starting work had actually added some extra damage to the car that could have been avoided. (Author's collection)

plenty of soapy water and go slowly in a small area. If you find 1200 isn't really working, switch to 1000, then 800, then 600 progressively, but always go back up to a fine grit when you're 80% of the way through the final layer of paint – so many stripped cars bear witness to too coarse a grit of paper being used in the stripping process. Once you've put deep scratches in the original paint, or sanded through the original paint to the primer, there really is no going back.

Rather than using just wet and dry paper with your fingers, use the paper folded around a foam backing pad – this will lessen the risk of burning through the paint where your finger tips are putting pressure on the panel most. You may think it looks cool with more primer showing, but sanding through to primer will always look unnatural.

5. Razor blades
Using plastic or steel razor blades to carefully chip

Whilst the black and orange layers came off very easily with thinners, the white layer was a completely different type of paint; fortunately, thinners and very fine steel wool took off the white without damaging the original paint underneath. (Author's collection)

It can be good for morale to strip one small area completely back to original paint as you go along. Generally, the rest of the paint was stripped off in layers, but doing one small area was helpful for inspiration. (Author's collection)

Sometimes, even when you expect that a car is original underneath, you'll be thrown a few curveballs: neither of the front wings on this car were original to the car, so both needed to be colour matched. (Author's collection)

Even if you get lucky with thinners, paint stripping an entire car is still a very laborious process; the paint was so thick on this car that a paintbrush was used to work the thinners into the paint, before wiping off with a cloth. Lots of cloths were needed, as well as refreshing the thinners on a regular basis. (Author's collection)

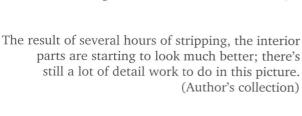

The result of several hours of stripping, the interior parts are starting to look much better; there's still a lot of detail work to do in this picture. (Author's collection)

Quite often, when cars were repainted on the outside, the inside will have been matched too; stripping intricate interior parts is a very time-consuming process. (Author's collection)

In some extreme cases, people will even paint vinyl upholstery. This isn't the first VW interior that I have had to strip paint from to get back to original. (Author's collection)

to clean the surface thoroughly. Cleaning involves soap and water, usually a kitchen green scourer or mild Scotch-Brite pad and plenty of elbow grease. Once you have thoroughly cleaned the area until the water runs clear, you will still need to clean with a silicone remover type chemical and use thinners or a good quality panel wipe to ready the surface for paint. Although many clearcoated cars look like they have been painted in heavy coats, this is the last thing you should do – if you paint in heavy coats and don't bake each coat after application, the outside of the lacquer will likely dry quicker than the inside layers do, which will eventually result in cracking.

Love it or loathe it, there's no denying that clearcoat, as here on Austin Working's '68, gives a car a look like no other, especially those that have a good degree of surface rust covering the remaining primer. Clearcoating rust darkens this, and gives it a deep shine – no other product will make surface rust shine like this. (Courtesy Andrew Thompson/AThompsonsPhoto)

off paint really is a last resort – it's extremely likely, especially with steel razor blades, that you will go through the original paint to the primer or bare metal in several areas. The decision as to whether to keep going or not really is up to you – there comes a point when you either need to decide to put up with paint that looks really bad or to blend in the paint or repaint the whole car.

Clearcoating

Many people like the look of clearcoated Patina – it gives a look like no other, Patinated and rusty, but shiny at the same time. The issue that many others have with clearcoat, is that it will eventually fail and may ruin the original paint underneath. When it comes to living with a hardcore Patina car in a damp climate, clearcoat will definitely halt the process of rusting for quite some time, but there are many pitfalls when it comes to applying it in the first place – it's not just a simple idea of blasting it on and letting it dry.

Before you can apply any clearcoat, you will need

As far as which products to use, don't even think about modern water-based cellulose or rattle can lacquer – this never really dries properly and will be easily damaged by fuel spills, bird mess and is very prone to scratches. 2k lacquer will need to be applied in a spray booth and oven-baked between coats but really is the only choice. Depending on your preference, you can opt for gloss, satin or matt lacquer. Once it is fully dried, you can wet sand and buff as you would with any regular paint finish. The beauty of 2k lacquer is that it has a hardener mixed in, so should dry better under the surface.

Many people assume you can just spray clearcoat straight over rust, but to do so would cause the paint to not adhere correctly. The surface of the body will first need to be scrubbed with a green scourer pad and hot soapy water until the water runs clear, followed by using panel wipe. Depending on which product you use, there can still be issues with the clearcoat not adhering to the surface properly. (Courtesy Andrew Thompson/AThompsonsPhoto)

Before committing to clearcoat, it may be worth machine polishing the car to see how it comes out; even original VW primer and, to a degree, the surface rust, will take on a shine. This is my '68 Sunroof after a machine polish, the beer wasn't used in the buffing process, but did make the prospect of tackling the job a little easier. (Author's collection)

Surface treatments

Before you read the following section, it's worth mentioning that, whatever surface treatment you decide on, you really need to make the decision now and stick to it: once you've applied clearcoat or boiled linseed oil, there is no going back. The one thing that is less of a commitment is giving the car a few coats of wax. The only problem that wax will cause if you then decide to clearcoat, is that it will likely be a pain trying to remove all of the silicone from the paintwork – if you don't do this, then you'll get fisheyes in the paint, or other silicone-based reactions.

1. Wax

There are hundreds of car wax products on the market and many of them are described as wax polish. Many of these products contain some kind of mild abrasive compound to get rid of oxidation, so be very careful what you buy – if you wish to preserve a dull, faded original finish and not get a car to shine, then you'll need to be careful to apply only natural wax products with no abrasive polymers in. If you want a semi-gloss sheen on a car that you're not buffing, then using a wax polish with some mild abrasive will work to give this kind of look.

I applied several coats of wax to my '68 Sunroof Beetle, but found that the damp, salty air near the beach where I live would still bring back the rusting in a matter of a few days. Ultimately, I chose to apply some clearcoat to the roof. (Author's collection)

You'd be surprised how removing the dead, old paint by buffing with a compound will restore most paint finishes virtually to showroom condition, especially once a few coats of carnauba wax are added. (Author's collection)

2. Buffing

Buffing can either be done by hand or by machine – a greater shine will be achieved with a machine, but it will remove more layers of paint in doing so. Many different companies offer liquid compounds – I've personally had success with Farecla G3, 3M Fast Cut Plus, Cartek, and Meguiars products. There are varying degrees of abrasives in each product, with most manufacturers selling a more abrasive liquid compound for initial buffing and a milder abrasive for

My '68 Sunroof Beetle the day I got home from Germany with it; the car had been sitting outside for around three years, so needed careful cleaning before the paint could be polished; as you can see, the paint is very dull and chalky, with some mould. (Author's collection)

Thoroughly washing the car before, during and after the buffing process. (Author's collection)

Buffing is carried out in several stages, with a minimum of two passes with the machine buffer. The smaller sections are detailed by hand, though small air-powered machine buffers are available. (Author's collection)

finishing. When you're buying a specific manufacturer's products, keep in mind that they may be better if used with their own application pads.

As with all methods, start out with the least abrasive and work backwards. In extreme cases, or with certain deep colours, you may have to wet sand with 2000, 1500 or 1200 wet and dry first, in order to remove thick layers of dead paint from the surface. If you are wet sanding, then finishing with 2000-3000 grit or

higher will produce a better end result without fine surface scratches.

3. Boiled linseed oil
Boiled linseed oil has become popular in Patina car circles more recently – it leaves the surface slightly tacky and needs re-applying every couple of months. Whilst it brings a deeper colour and light sheen to a Patina paint finish, it is very difficult to ever remove

The same car after being polished and lowered with a 4in narrowed beam and drop spindles. (Author's collection)

properly once it's been applied. Along with clearcoat, this is another product that can actually damage the Patina paint finish in the long-term. It is also very volatile and, if not handled or stored correctly, can self combust – be particularly careful with rags once you've finished applying.

4. Ankor wax
Ankor wax is a thin waxy coating that can be sprayed onto the paint finish – it protects from the elements, but remains sticky. Whilst the viscosity makes it really good for seeping into every single tight nook, cranny and body seam, it attracts dirt and will make your ride look more rat than Patina. The only way to clean off the dirt is to remove the product with a degreaser and start again. This is another product that doesn't really enhance the finish – you lose more in the dirt it attracts than you gain with the deeper colour and satin sheen it gives.

Summary

When it comes down to it, the actual Patina and paint finish on your car are one of the, if not **the** most important aspect of getting it right with a Patina car. Whether it's an original survivor car or one that needs a ton of work to appear like a survivor, there's a lot at stake and a lot to think about before you dive in and start making decisions. Research and practice are key to making whatever you're working on look like it's a survivor, versus a badly faked fauxtina car.

Boiled linseed oil will seal the rust, add a light sheen, and darken the rust slightly, as here on Bobby Willcox' car. (Author's collection)

CHAPTER SIX
Suspension modifications

Back in the days when the Patina VW scene was fairly new, 99 per cent of the Patina cars that would ever see the light of day would be lowered in some way. Around the early to mid-2000s, the narrowed front beam craze kicked off and, like it or not, no one could deny that a lowered car with a seriously narrowed front beam had a really radical look. What followed was a competition, with many people determined to build the lowest car with the most radical suspension modifications.

Whilst many of these modifications were based on out-of-the-box thinking that pushed boundaries, or set examples for others to copy, what was not really thought about was how the finished cars would drive, and whether they'd be permanently devalued as a result of the modifications and resulting damage from being driven too low, with little to almost no ground clearance. In the past five years, there's been a bigger emergence of stock height Patina cars coming onto the scene. Some of these owners have owned seriously slammed cars before, others may not have, but it's now seen as more acceptable to keep a car stock height or raise the suspension for an off-road look.

Many people think that a car has to be standard height or completely slammed, but a mild drop works, too. I built this Savannah Beige '69 Deluxe a few years ago – this picture is before the front height was brought down another inch or two. This Bus featured a 4in narrowed link pin beam with drop spindles and adjustable spring plates. (Author's collection)

This is the other extreme. Built by Type 2 Detectives and now in The Netherlands, it takes a huge amount of work to get a Bus this low.
(Courtesy Joss Ashley)

If you're looking to build a 'toy' that gets minimal use and you're prepared to live with the limitations of a lowered or modified car, then go for it, but it definitely pays to have a good think about what your intended uses are. Many of the stock height or raised cars and Buses that are around now are owned by people who've lived the lowered life and now want to drive something that isn't limited to smooth tarmac. Many people also maybe regret cutting into a survivor car and don't want to do it again – I know many people, myself included, who don't even like drilling new holes in the floor of a survivor Camper to screw in new furniture.

Of course, there is a balance between stock and slammed to the floor and this is a vehicle that is lowered enough that it looks good, but also functions correctly and doesn't bottom out or hit the floor. When it comes down to it, lowering a car in this manner is just nuts and bolts – it's bolting on some different suspension parts and retaining the original parts for future use, should the need arise. Many people, on the grounds of cost, decide to first get a car on the road stock height and then lower it later if they decide to – this is much cheaper and quicker in terms of build cost, dependent on whether you later decide to upgrade the brakes and suspension as well – you could end up spending out twice in the long run.

Having built a lot of slammed Volkswagens through my old company, The Bus Station (2002-2013), I figured out a long time ago what works when it comes to having a cool looking, but perfectly usable, static slammed Patina Volkswagen. Whether it's a Bug, Bus, Karmann Ghia, or Type 3 you're looking to build, this chapter is the Patina Volkswagen recipe, the path to getting suspension modifications spot on so you're not breaking things as you drive. Of course, you could always fit air ride or hydraulic suspension; I have never done this, as I know too many people who have done so and are constantly fixing problems. I feel that air ride is just so much more to go wrong, but that doesn't stop you doing it – each to their own.

Before we go any further, it should be established that modifying anything has its drawbacks; there's a domino effect – if you modify one thing, then usually several other things will also need to be modified, in order to make things work correctly. The problem with a lot of slammed Volkswagens out there – especially in countries where there are no annual inspection laws – is that often the bare minimum is done, in order

I built this '62 Single Cab as a shop truck and rolling advertisement for my old business, The Bus Station. It featured a 4in narrowed, 7-degree caster front beam with flipped spindles, owner-built straight axle rear, as well as tie rod notches, and a raised steering box. The added caster helped it to track straight, even at speed. (Author's collection)

I'm sure a few people thought Jason Reich was crazy when he bought this car as an already built and very nice looking car, then stripped it and took off the body. What resulted was a year-long build to show quality. The suspension features a 4in narrowed beam and Porsche Fuchs wheels in 4.5inx15in/6inx15in (front/rear). (Courtesy Jason Reich/Aircooled Vintage Works)

One of Jason's previous builds, this '58 Ragtop is now in Belgium; the car featured a 4in narrowed beam, two outer spline rear drop, and original steel EMPI Sprintstar wheels. (Courtesy Jason Reich/ Aircooled Vintage Works)

One of my all-time favourites, Jason's Barndoor era Single Cab features original Ansen Sprint wheels and was his daily driver for over a year. (Courtesy Jason Reich/Aircooled Vintage Works)

Built in the early days of the Patina scene and the first car in Sweden to be the subject of a full body-off Patina build, Martin

Henriksson's Oval Beetle features American Eagle five-spoke wheels. (Courtesy Martin Henriksson)

Mid-way through narrowing a Split Bus lower trailing arm shock mount; this allows the shock absorber to sit vertically on 4in narrowed beams. Every modification you make has a knock-on effect on other components. (Author's collection)

to make a car look slammed, but on the tightest of budgets. This, naturally, gives lowered Volkswagens a bad name.

Although there was a similar suspension guide in the *Patina Volkswagens* book, this focused solely on lowering the car as much as possible, whilst setting it up to ride well and still go around corners. This guide will cover that area too, as well as covering mild lowering options and suspension raising options too, for those who want the looks and functionality of off-road driving.

Disclaimer: When it comes to modifying any car suspension, please take advice from various sources and don't try to do it yourself if you don't have the capabilities – modifying the suspension on a car isn't a good place to learn mechanics or welding, and it isn't a good place to make (potentially life-threatening) mistakes. When planning and buying suspension products for your car, please also take into account the road traffic laws in your country. Some countries won't allow steering or suspension parts that have been welded for example, even if that welding is on a forged steel part and is carried out to a high standard.

First things first – wheel choice

When it comes to working out the stance of your car and how to achieve it, you will first need to make a wheel choice; a front beam that might work perfectly well with 4.5x15in Fuchs wheels, for example, won't work too well if you then change your mind and decide to fit 7x17in BRM style wheels, or even 15in Randars with a completely different offset. Figuring out the ET (offset) figure of the wheel you are planning to use first, the backspacing figure, will save a lot of headaches later when you've spent a lot of

The only vehicle I have ever bought that was already lowered, it took a fair bit of trial and error to raise the original paint '67 Kombi up a little and figure out the best wheel and tyre combination to work with the suspension setup. At this kind of height and with the great offset of the chrome Sprintstar wheels, the Bus would look better with a 2in narrowed beam than a 4in one. (Author's collection)

As an example of building a car around the wheel choice, I designed the entire suspension setup on Timothy Drayson's '66 SO42 Westy to accommodate the Rocket Racing wheels, designed for American Muscle Cars. The front featured a 6in narrowed beam, which bolted up to the inside of the chassis rails, the rear featuring a short axle setup with a narrowed torsion housing. (Author's collection)

money and time and the tyres rub, or the turning circle is hopeless.

Although a lot of people assume that a front beam looks better when it is really tucked, there are optimal amounts to narrow a front beam in order for the tyres to clear on both steering locks and for the wheel to sit in the optimal part of the inner wheelarch area, clearing things like inner wheelarch lips. Some people

Chase Hill's Beetle was built around a set of Porsche pattern Cosmic wheels, and features a 4in narrowed beam. Fat rear tyres have become more popular since being adopted by the German Folks Klub many years ago. (Courtesy Chase Hill/Cage66)

Whilst many choose to run new aftermarket wheels, a few track down original period performance wheels from back in the day. These are all four-lug to suit the late Beetle/Karmann Ghia/Type 3. (Courtesy Chadd Magee)

Porsche Fuchs, as fitted to Steve Parsons' '67 Beetle, are a popular choice, as they look so good. They also have a great offset – tucking in nicely. Many other types of wheels would necessitate a different suspension setup. (Courtesy Steve Parsons)

don't really like the tucked look either, so the aim of this chapter is to explore a few different looks and how to achieve them.

When it comes to the Karmann Ghia, there's a bit more width up front to play with, so you may want to carry out some measurements (or search the forums at thesamba.com to see what others have done) and go with a slightly less-narrow beam than if you had a Bug.

Type 1 – Bug and Karmann Ghia

While there are hundreds of possible suspension configurations to take into consideration when building a raised, mildly lowered, or slammed Bug, many of them only ever make a car look good; but the aim should be to make a Bug look good **and** drive well. It's all well and good running a seriously narrowed front axle beam, for instance, but what does that translate to when you try and steer the car around a tight corner? Similarly, when it comes to the rear suspension, it's one thing to lower or raise a car 6in at the rear, but how does that compute with tyre and gearbox wear?

Going low – front suspension

Using Fuchs style wheels as an example (the same would work for Cosmics or Gas Burner style wheels), a 4in narrowed front beam is something you can buy off the shelf and is really the best possible compromise for a narrow look and decent turning circle when

Brett Elsmore likes the tucked look. He fitted an 8in narrowed beam to his Karmann Ghia, and alternates between 15in Porsche pattern Cosmic wheels and 17in New Beetle BRM wheels. (Courtesy Brett Elsmore/ OB1Brand)

combined with drop spindles. Let's just say here; fitting a narrowed beam without drop spindles and trying to go low just won't work, as when you try and go low using lowering adjusters alone, the wheel and tyre will sit way too far forwards; the trailing arms of the front axle beam work in an arc, so the lower you go on adjusters also means the wheel is moving further and further forwards.

Fitting drop spindles, although they do increase the front track width ⅝in or around 9mm per side, gives you an immediate 2.5in drop on a Type 1 beam, without negatively affecting either the ride quality or steering geometry. Of course, if you don't plan on a really tucked look, you will still need a 2in narrowed front beam if you are fitting drop spindles, in order to

correct the track width increase of the drop spindles. Once you have your narrowed beam and drop spindles fitted, there are other options to take into account when it comes to setting up the car to drive well.

Tyre options on the front of really low Type 1s are numerous – some people will go for the smallest Smart car tyres possible, such as a 165/50/15 but on anything but a completely slammed car these will look ridiculous, as there will be too much wheelarch gap around the tyre. Many people's tyre of choice for the front of a fairly low Type 1 is a 145/65/15 tyre, or if you're looking for something a bit wider for more grip and better handling, a 165/60/15 – it gives a similar sidewall height as the 145/65 but more contact on the road.

John Jones at Colorado-based Kustom Coach Werks (KCW) built this mildly lowered '66 Beetle for his son Zack. The car had been bought for $500 by Jesse Worley in Glenwood Springs. (Courtesy John Jones/ Kustom Coach Werks)

Mildly lowered front suspension – Type 1 cars

If you just want to lower the front of your car a little, but not a huge amount and aren't concerned about the major tuck of a narrowed beam, then there are a few options. As mentioned above, a 2in narrowed beam and drop spindles paired will give a just-narrower-than-stock look, which is better if you plan to run taller profile tyres; the old Cal Look favourites such as 135/80/15 or 145/80/15 work well with this setup for a more traditional look. A real rookie mistake that many make is to fit drop spindles without narrowing the front beam – this will give almost 2in of track width increase, so even if you are running original wheels, the front suspension will look too wide. Drop spindles on a Type 1 should only ever be fitted with a narrowed beam.

Another option for those wanting an original look with whitewall Crossply/Bias Ply tyres, but

Note the clear difference between Zack's mildly lowered car and Franz Muhr's old slammed car, parked behind. Zack's car features a 2in narrowed beam and one spline rear drop: a good compromise if you want to drive a Beetle daily over rough roads. (Courtesy Franz Muhr/Kustom Coach Werks)

Extending the steering arm on my '68 Sunroof; this restores the short tie rod angle to correct Ackerman by cutting off this part and extending it. It needs to be tackled by a professional welder. Russell Ludwig at Old Speed in Paramount, California, offers similar welded versions of this drop arm, but you'll need to check the road regulations in your country before deciding to run a welded steering drop arm. Australian company Fresh Kustoms now offers brand new CNC machined arms. (Author's collection)

Another product worth considering if you're planning to go with a narrowed beam and drop spindles. Chase Hill produces extended trailing arms: these make the front wheel sit back further in the wheelarch, centering the wheel for aesthetics purposes and making the tyre less prone to hitting the headlight bucket. Chase manufactures the upper trailing arm in a way that also increases shock absorber clearance. (Courtesy Chase Hill)

a bit lower than standard is to fit a 2in narrowed front beam but without fitting drop spindles. As the original style tyres are much taller and skinnier than tyres you would normally fit on a lowered car, it will be necessary to narrow the beam by 2in to aid with tyre clearance. This can be paired with a one outer spline drop at the rear for a nice 2in drop all round, but with a vintage look that keeps people guessing.

Setting up front suspension

The first thing you should always fit when lowering the front suspension of a Type 1 car is caster shims. These fit between the lower beam tube and the frame head of the car, pushing the lower beam tube out further than the upper beam tube. Caster shims were designed to restore stability when the front of the car was lower than the back of the car, but are good to aid stability on all lowered type 1 cars.

It should go without saying that the tracking or

Preparing the 4in narrowed Aire Valley beam to go into my '68 Sunroof Beetle. (Author's collection)

alignment will need to be checked by a competent garage, You will, however, need to set it up somewhere close before you drive the car anywhere. Before you check the tracking, you'll need to make sure that the steering box is centred – if you skip this step, you will be left with a car that wanders all over the road.

For cars with front suspension narrowed more than 2-3in, you will need to do some kind of correction of the Ackerman angle. As you narrow the front suspension beyond 2-3in, the angle of the tie rods changes. This is not such a problem with the long tie rod, but it can become a major problem with the short tie rod; this will begin to push backwards, rather than outwards, making the outer front wheel unable to turn enough on corners.

Correcting this issue can be difficult and there are usually compromises with whatever method you choose. Fitting a quick steer kit will help, but as it removes one whole turn from the steering lock, it can make the car feel more skittish. Some people have another tapered hole made in the Pitman arm of the spindle, but the method I've found the most success with is to extend the area of the steering box drop arm where the short tie rod goes. Old Speed in California offers a welded option or, more recently, an Australian company called Fresh Kustoms have begun manufacturing a new extended Pitman arm from scratch.

For the rough alignment, I use a large and small steel rule to get the tracking somewhere near, by measuring against the wheel rim at a point towards the rear of the wheel, then a point as close toward the front of the car as possible. The front measurement should be 1-5mm less than the back, so the alignment is slightly toe in. The weight of the car must be on the wheels for this – suspension compressed.

I had always liked late Bugs, but it was seeing Dave Eadon's '72 at Volksworld Show 2012 that inspired me to buy and build the '68 Sunroof car. (Courtesy Joss Ashley)

Ball joint cars (1966 onwards) have the beam tubes spaced wider apart, meaning the frame head also sits lower at the front of the floorpan; going really low on these cars is harder. You can trim off the excess metal that sits below the weld on the front of the frame head, as well as trimming and re-ending the lower adjuster bolt to give extra ground clearance. When assembling each spindle to the trailing arms on ball joint cars, you should always set the camber with the concentric camber adjusting nut on the upper ball joint; the notch in the nut should face forwards when the wheel faces forwards for initial setup – the alignment shop will adjust from there.

My finished '68 Sunroof car; it featured a 4in narrowed beam, drop spindles, and the rear suspension setup for a 3in drop. The bolt pattern was changed to Porsche 5x130, and a set of bargain-priced repro Cosmic wheels were bolted on. Tyres were 165/65/15 front and 185/65/15 rear. (Author's collection)

It's hard to get a specific drop without using a magnetic angle finder/inclinometer. Doing so will help fine-tune the height. (Author's collection)

When it comes to narrowed front beams, try to buy a beam with high-quality bushes or bearings, as many of the urethane type bushes wear quickly, causing problems with ride quality and safety. With some ingenuity, even beams of 5-6in narrowed can be fitted with shock towers. There's an age-old debate going on, especially in the USA, about the use of narrowed beams without shock towers; some argue that the resultant increase in springing rate from narrowing the torsion bars inside the beam negates the use of shock absorbers/dampers.

While there may be some that have set up a beam like this and are satisfied with it, the use of shock absorbers is necessary to damp the springing action of the suspension. Countries with inspection laws will all require shocks to be fitted and even in those areas without an inspection, shock absorbers make sound sense from an engineering point of view. The best advice is to run oil-filled shocks at the front of the car, due to the excessive choppiness of gas shocks when it comes to ride quality.

Rear suspension

When it comes to the rear suspension, it is possible to just lower a car by turning the spring plates on the rear torsion bars – one outer spline gives approximately 2in of adjustment, whereas one inner spline gives around 2.5in. By using the inner and outer splines, it is possible to raise or lower a car by any precise amount. Buy a magnetic angle finder or inclinometer for this job and you can work it out easier; 4° of adjustment equals one inch in height change.

If you lower the suspension using this method, you will be best to fit gas shocks on the rear; turning the spring plates on the splines results in a loss of preload

in the rear torsion bars, making the rear suspension excessively soft. If you are lowering more than one inner spline (2.5in) you will also need to notch the spring plate adjacent to the stop along the upper edge; do this in a gentle radiused curve, as spring steel is more brittle than normal steel and more prone to sudden failure.

Lowering the rear of the car using the above method works fine, to a degree, but do be aware that the lower you go with this method, the more the rear suspension will toe in, making handling and tyre wear a serious issue.

By far a better method of lowering the rear is to use extended drop spring plate – these are also available as adjustable spring plates. These plates are longer to correct the toe issues when lowering on just the splines, and will help with better handling and lower tyre wear.

Raising Type 1 cars

If you're planning on raising a type 1 car, then it's worth checking out some VW off-road forums to see what a lot of the Baja guys are doing with their cars. If you're doing a full body-off build anyway, then a body lift kit is one way to raise you your car without changing the suspension geometry – these are generally available in 2-3in options.

1. Pre-'66 link pin cars – front

With early cars, you either have the option of raised spindles or adjusters welded into the front beam. Depending on how much you are planning to raise the car and how good you want the ride quality to be, using raised spindles may be a good idea, even if it is a more expensive option. If you raise the car too

Franz Muhr's old raised '66 Beetle had a combination of a body lift and type 181 arms and spindles. Due to the wider aggressive tyres, 15in Bus wheels were used. Franz has always built the cars *he* wants, regardless of current tastes. (Courtesy Franz Muhr/ Kustom Coach Werks)

much on adjusters, the torsion leaves in the beam will be working in the wrong configuration and will have little to no spring.

Patrick Peet's survivor Baja was raised on the rear splines, with adjusters in the front beam. Beware that adjusters welded into the front beam can weaken it for off-road use. (Author's collection)

2. Post-'66 ball joint cars – front

By far the best way to raise the front of a ball joint car is to find a set of front arms and spindles from a Trekker/Thing/Type 181/2 – on these cars, both ball joints face downwards, where on a regular type 1 car they are opposing; you'll need the arms and spindles but can expect a bolt-on, 2.5-3in raise.

3. Swing axle cars – rear

On swing axle cars, you can adjust the rear suspension on the splines, as you would when lowering. You will have to get the spring plate back on the stop though, which can be difficult. Warning: The spring plate, even at the stock position, has a strong preload – if you get in the way of it and it suddenly jumps off the stop, it will break bones.

The second option for swing axle rear suspension is to fit a reduction hub setup from a Split Screen Bus, or an early Type 181/2 – this gives 3.5in of lift but does reduce high-speed gearing. It will also require that you modify the spring plates.

4. Independent Rear Suspension cars – rear

Independent Rear Suspension (IRS) Cars can also be raised on the splines, but even at around the 2in raise point, you'll find that the Constant Velocity (CV) joints begin to run out of travel. Type 1 CVs have an angle of 12°, compared to the Type 2 with a 17° angle. Type 181/Porsche 944 CVs are better still at 22°, or if you're really reaching for the sky, Porsche 930 CVs have a 25° angle; the last 3° is where the money is though, as 930 CVs are very expensive. There's a great CV joint 101 at www.blindchickenracing.com. With anything other than the stock Bug CVs, you'll need to also swap to larger drive flanges and, in the case of the 930 CVs, different driveshafts.

Type 2 – Bus – Split Screen

Lowering a Split Screen Type 2 is far more complicated, with far more options than any of the other models. Years ago, people used to fit a Bay Window Bus front axle beam to Split Buses, especially in Europe; 1968-69 ball joint beams bolt right up to the Split Bus chassis rails, unlike later, 1970 onwards, ball joint beams. The main issues with fitting a ball joint beam to a Split Bus if you're planning to go low, is that they sit 1-2in higher than a link pin Split Bus beam and the track width is 66mm wider; clearly no good if you're looking to narrow the front suspension, but great if you're looking to raise the suspension.

Craig Yelley built this lowered '58 Bus for a friend in the UK; the BTR wheels require a narrower setup on the rear than a regular straight axle.
(Courtesy Craig Yelley/Vintage VW)

Front suspension

When it comes to lowering the front of a Split Bus, the age-old recipe is to narrow the front beam by 4in and fit 'flipped' drop spindles. Just because this is an age-old recipe though, doesn't mean it's the right thing to do for you and your Bus. Although people like the uber tucked look that a 4in narrowed beam gives, going 4in

narrowed with some wheels will give you more tyre clearance issues than if you went for a 2in narrowed beam.

Standard steel wheels and wheels with a tucked offset like Porsche Fuchs style wheels will sit in the sweet spot in the wheel well with a 2in narrowed beam, whereas with a 4in beam you will have to tub the inner arches to get the Bus to sit as low. Of course, if you plan to run wheels with a lower ET figure, like Randar wheels, BRM, or EMPI 5 spoke types, then a 4in narrowed beam may be better for you.

Flipped spindles seem to have become the industry standard in the last ten to 15 years and it's easy to see why: they can be built by anyone with moderate skills and are not two spindles welded together, which seems to scare people even when carried out professionally. The main issues when it comes to flipped spindles, though, are that they mess up the caster angle, and run only a single thrust surface rather than the double thrust of stock height spindles. There's also the issue of the tie rods hitting the chassis with flipped spindles, as the pitman arm sits higher up the spindle in relation to stock; very low Buses with flipped spindles will need the chassis to be notched for clearance.

When it comes to welded drop spindles, especially ones from a reputable shop like Old Speed or Wagenswest, they run dual thrust faces like a standard spindle and don't mess up the caster angle. The pitman arm will also sit in the stock location with these spindles, so you won't need to notch the chassis. They really do make a lot of sense over flipped spindles, but the welding aspect scares most people off. So, what's the solution to correct the caster angle when running flipped spindles? A beam with caster correction built-in.

When I ran The Bus Station Slammin' Shop (TBS), we experimented a lot on Bus beams when it came to caster correction; with a Bus beam, it isn't a simple case of fitting caster shims, but the caster correction has to be built into the structure of the beam. At TBS, we settled on 7° of caster correction on TBS scratch-built Bus narrowed beams and it gave great stability at speed; I once took a one-minute video of my '62 Single Cab going die-straight down the highway with both hands off the steering wheel. This is in stark comparison with off the shelf narrowed Bus beams at the time used by most other companies, which needed constant correction of the steering on the highway to keep the Bus in a straight line.

When it comes to buying a Bus beam with in-built caster correction these days, the guys at Dog Back Performance in Germany and Transporterhaus in the UK seem to have the market cornered; their beams come with concentric caster adjustment nuts around

A 4in narrowed front beam, such as the one on Steven Kretschmar's hardcore Patina Sea Blue Standard, has become the basic norm for lowering a Split Bus and giving it a radical look. (Author's collection)

Notching the spring plates becomes necessary when lowering more than 2-3in. A nice graduated curve is the way to go when notching: a sharp angle is more likely to fracture. (Author's collection)

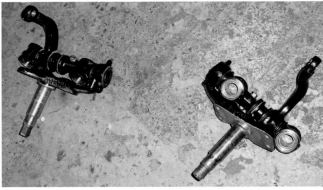

Flipped drop spindles are built by changing the inclination of the kingpin in relation to the spindle body. They give a 3-3.5in drop whilst preserving the factory ride quality. (Author's collection)

Getting a Bus like Kenny Davis' Standard Microbus this low takes a substantial amount of effort; lowering a Split Bus right is a lot more involved than any other model. (Courtesy Kenny Davis)

The perfect answer to setting up the correct caster angle on a narrowed Bus beam, Dogback Performance beams are manufactured with eccentric caster adjusters around the mounting bolt holes. (Courtesy James Peene)

the mounting bolts, much like the camber nuts on the upper ball joint of late-model Volkswagens. Bear in mind that there is a compromise with these beams though, in that the steering idler arm will also change angle when you adjust the caster.

The other modification that needs to be made on a 4in narrowed beam is to narrow the lower shock absorber mount on the front trailing arms – this needs to be narrowed in order for the shock absorber to sit at the correct angle. If you choose not to do this, not only will the shock sit at an angle, putting a strain on the rubber bushes, but it will also foul the beam mounting bolts on most beams.

The last modification that needs mentioning here when it comes to narrowed axle beams is the steering centre pin. On some off-the-shelf narrowed Bus beams and on stock beams, the Split Bus centre pin sits around 1in lower than the centre steering pin housing on the beam. If you want to reduce the chances of hitting anything in the road though, this really needs to be raised up flush to the bottom of the housing; the pin will also need to be shortened and re-notched and the lower bush driven further in.

Steering box raise

Even when it comes to running a sensible height on a lowered and narrowed Bus, the steering box will be too low to the ground. In order to stop the steering box hitting, many people choose to raise the steering box. Raising the steering box around 1.5in can be done

'Fire Bus Phil' Jarvis runs his original Split Screen German Fire Bus on the drag strip with some pretty impressive times; setting any VW up to race is not as simple as carrying out 'regular' lowering. Phil's Bus features a 2387cc Type 1 engine, and covers the quarter-mile in just over 11 seconds at almost 120mph. (Courtesy Julian Hunt)

Raising the centre pin housing on a Bus beam for extra ground clearance, this also requires shortening and re-notching the pin. (Author's collection)

without any modifications to the cab floor. There are laser cut and folded steering box raise kits available if you're not keen on cutting and welding the chassis section where the steering box bolts up; the standard raise on these is 42mm, which does necessitate a slight bulge to be fabricated in the cab floor. These, along with a new, higher clearance pedal arm are available through Hayburner (www.hayburner.co.uk).

If you don't want to 'hack' your Bus and raise the

A fully refurbished late Beetle gearbox ready to fit into my old 1962 Single Cab Pickup. (Author's collection)

steering box, you could fit one of the available steering rack kits on the market. In my experience, the most popular brand tends to give the steering a very tight feel, though, and need endless minor correction when driving. Like I said earlier, any modification you make will have a knock-on effect in other areas, and sometimes compromises have to be made. If it were my choice, I would always keep the factory steering box.

Mid-way through fitting a 42mm steering box raise chassis section on my '62 Single Cab. (Author's collection)

Rear suspension

From the factory, Split Screen Buses came with reduction boxes at the ends of the rear axle tubes, effectively raising the ground clearance by 3.5in. Going any lower than a couple of inches at the rear on a Split Bus means getting rid of the reduction boxes – there are two basic methods of doing this, but there are a lot of options when it comes to the actual parts you can use and kits that are available.

The main reasons to get rid of the reduction boxes when going low are: as the oil supply to the reduction boxes needs to run down the axle tubes from the gearbox, lowering a Bus to the point that the axle tubes are at a higher angle means that this oil supply will be interrupted; and lowering more than a couple of inches will result in excessive rear wheel camber, which will cause the bearings and gears to wear at a faster rate.

A third good reason to get rid of the reductions on lowered Buses is the gearing. Reduction boxes were employed by Volkswagen on the 1st generation Transporter as a way of making a fully-loaded 25hp Bus go up steep hills. As engine size and spec increased, this raised gearing was less necessary; most Split Buses these days are running at least double this original horsepower.

When it comes to getting rid of the reduction boxes, there are two main methods to use: Straight Axle and Independent Rear Suspension (IRS). Although there are just two methods, there are several ways of carrying out the modifications, with a wealth of different kits and parts for either method.

Straight axle

Generally accepted as the best method for going low, doing a straight axle conversion on your Bus will mean lowering the rear a minimum of 3.5in. Many people use Bug gearboxes when doing this, but it is also possible to flip the differential in your standard gearbox (not flipping the diff will cause you to have four reverse gears and one forward gear).

Traditionally, straight axle kits would consist of modified spring plates and custom length axle tubes running early short end castings with extended tubes. You would also need to source early bearing caps and long axles. A few years ago though, a few different people came up with the adapter style kit. With this type kit, you could simply bolt in a long or short axle gearbox complete with original axles and tubes; the adapter kit consists of spacers to space the mounting flanges for the axle tubes inboard of the spring plates.

There's a fair bit of snobbery around when it comes to original style or adapter kit; I've used both when running The Bus Station, and I found the adapter kit perfectly adequate and reliable in the Buses I used it on – it also came in at a lower cost and required less work to fit. The adapter kits use either 1968-69 Bay Window spring plates, or cut down and re-drilled Split Bus spring plates.

There is a third method to employ when straight axling a Split Bus: you can narrow the rear torsion housing, and fit up any short or long axle gearbox complete. This method is much more invasive and harder to return a Bus back to stock if it is carried out, but it works well especially if you plan to run much wider rear wheels; you can get the same outcome with an adapter kit with short axles though, so cutting and narrowing the rear torsion housing isn't really necessary.

Independent rear suspension (IRS)

When it comes to most IRS kits, you can run at stock height or a mild suspension drop. IRS is also suitable for airbag suspension, but usually, the kits and the Bus need substantial modification for this to happen. When it comes to IRS kits, the main distinction to make is whether you want to use Bay Window Bus parts or Beetle IRS parts.

Running an IRS setup at stock height necessitates the use of Type 181/Porsche 944 CV joints for an increased operating angle. (Author's collection)

1. Bay Window-based kits

There are a few different Bay Window-based kits out there, which use modified Bay Window trailing arms and spring plates, as well as the Bay Window hubs and rear brakes. You can either go for bolt-on kits, which contain bolt-on torsion bar brackets, or weld-on kits. The bolt-on kits are generally better, as they allow you to correct the camber and alignment setup before welding.

There are also kits where the entire rear frame horns are removed and replaced with new ones. These kits are well thought out when it comes to alignment, etc, but make it very difficult to return a Bus to stock if ever this is required.

2. Beetle-based kits

Beetle-based kits require the use of the swing arms, hubs, and brakes from a Beetle, and are a little lighter than Bus-based kits. They also offer better/ less expensive brake options. This is especially so if you plan to run a custom bolt pattern, or change to a Porsche bolt pattern. The Beetle-based kits allow the use of late Bug brakes and hardware, larger Type 3 rear brakes, and even Porsche 944 rear disc brakes, or aftermarket disc brakes.

With either method of IRS conversion, adjustable spring plates or extended drop plates can be used. With the Bay Window-based kits, you can also run horseshoe plates to gain extra drop, although certain aftermarket wheels won't fit these, as they widen the rear track.

It's also possible to run stock height with IRS; if you're looking to keep a Split Bus stock height, but have the benefit of better gearing and handling and less noise while driving, then IRS makes a lot of sense. In order to run stock height with IRS though, you will need to run Type 181/182 'Thing' rear drive axles, flanges, and CV joints, as these have more travel.

Raising a Split Bus

If you're looking to raise a Split Bus, lifted front spindles are available from companies like Wagenswest – many people opt for spindles and adjusters, whilst keeping the reduction boxes (RGB) on the back, and raising the suspension by one spline. Any more than this and the transmission will need to be lowered – a big fabrication job, necessitating chopping the rear cradle. John Jones at Kustom Coach Werks (www. kustomcoachwerks.com) is working on a Triple RGB setup, and has gone as far as having a printed 3D

With aggressive tyres and a slight suspension raise, Bubba's Turkis Panel Camper is a go-anywhere vehicle. (Author's collection)

John Jones of Kustom Coach Werks in Grand Junction, Colorado, managed over 60 nights staying and travelling in his '55 'Pamper' in 2019. This picture was taken while I was road-tripping with him in 2018. (Author's collection)

model made so far – this would potentially raise the rear more without any compromise on ride quality. Many of the guys who are raising Buses are realising that a narrowed beam is actually a bonus on a raised Bus, due to centring the wheel in the wheel well.

Of course, it's also possible to raise the rear of a Split Bus that's been IRS converted, but you will need the Porsche 930 CV joints and drive flanges, otherwise your CV joints will be constantly binding. As mentioned earlier, the 930 CVs are a significant investment – around $1000 all-in, so this can put a real dent in a budget.

Type 2 – Bus – Bay Window
front suspension

As with the Split Screen Bus, there now seems to be a generally accepted way to lower a Bay Window Bus and still retain good ride quality. Until around ten years ago, most people lowering a Bay Window Bus would narrow the existing front beam. As Bay Window beams have needle roller bearings in the ends, they were always much harder to narrow correctly. With the bearings in the ends, the usual method to narrow a Bay beam was to make an offset cut in the centre of each beam tube and remove the required amount from the centre of the beam. In order to mount the narrower beam up to the chassis rails, the original shock towers would then need to be removed in their entirety, before new laser cut flat plates could be welded on.

As time went by and a few people began to convert to Split Screen/Link pin beams up front, complete with flipped drop spindles, this became the accepted method of narrowing and lowering the front of a Bay Window. The pros of doing a conversion like this are numerous: the Split Bus beam lowers the front of a Bay Window Bus 1-2in over a Bay/ball joint beam as standard; when you add flipped spindles (3.5in drop)

Steve Fields' 1971 Chianti Red Kombi has all the right modifications for a nice-driving lowered Bus: it features a narrowed link pin beam and some chassis notching. (Courtesy Steve Fields)

A small beam raise means that the beam will just sit closer to the floor under the seat stands of a Bay; every inch that you don't have to lower the Bus on lowering adjusters equals better ride quality.
(Courtesy Steve Fields)

you are already around 5in lower than stock, without compromising much ride quality – it's true that ball joint beams ride a little softer, but to go 5in lower, and only lose a little softness was inconceivable in years gone by. The beam tubes on a Split beam are also closer together, meaning more ground clearance.

Another one of the pros of using a Split Bus beam is that, even without narrowing the beam, the front track width is already 66mm narrower (around 2.5 inches). This means that much wider wheels or those with a bigger offset can be fitted when using a Split Beam. Flipped drop spindles narrow the track width a further 9mm per side, so even a stock width Split Bus beam fitted to a Bay with flipped spindles is 3in narrower than stock. Of course, many still choose to narrow a Split Bus beam when fitting to a Bay, to create the most radical look possible, but it isn't always the best method to employ in order to make everything fit well and work correctly.

There are quite a few Bay Window Buses out there with 4in narrowed Split beams fitted, that are also super-low and fitted with wheel tub extensions to accommodate the wheels and tyres at the required height. Many of these wouldn't need tubs if they had been narrowed a lesser amount and had the wheels sitting in the sweet spot inside the wheel well.

When it comes to fitting a Split beam to an early (1968/69) Bay Window, the front brake options are easy if you want to retain the wide 5 (5x205mm) bolt pattern. The only difference between 1964-67 and 1968-70 front brakes is the grease seal in the later drum is a different diameter. If you want to convert to Porsche bolt pattern on the early Split Bus spindles, you can use many of the available kits to fit early Porsche 944 non-turbo front discs. There are also kits available using Wilwood and other four-pot callipers.

If you are looking to fit a Split Bus beam to a 1970 Bus, then the brakes will be the same as for 1968 and 1969, but where the beam bolts up to the chassis will be different. Luckily, the manufacturers of narrowed link pin beams and end plates these days tend to put both sets of holes in the end plates, so they can be mounted into the 1970-79 chassis rails.

When it comes to front brake options on the 1971-79 Bay Window Buses, however, things are a little trickier. If you're looking to retain the original 5x112mm bolt pattern, you can buy Brazilian front spindles and have them made into flipped drop spindles; with the Brazilian spindles, you can run late 1973 onwards discs and

Fully detailed suspension parts, as on Steve Fields' Bus, are the hallmark of a quality build.
(Courtesy Steve Fields)

Carrying out some small chassis notches for the driveshafts on a 1969 Bay Window Bus; drop plates bolted between the swing arm and hub mean that the hub sits higher in relation to the swing arm. (Author's collection)

Dropped and adjustable spring plates mean that it's easier to fine-tune the ride height and get the rear wheels off. Make sure you buy extended versions to correct toe-in issues. (Author's collection)

callipers. Of course, you could retrofit drum brakes onto a later Bay Window Bus, but it really makes no sense to do so. You could fit a CSP disc kit to retain discs and convert to 5x130 or 5x205mm – some kits are supplied with a dual PCD option too.

Rear suspension

When it comes to lowering the rear suspension of the Bay Window, many simply lower by turning the spring plates a notch or two on the inner or outer splines. This is fine to a degree, but if you lower more than one spline using this method, the toe-in of the rear suspension will be excessive. It's better to use extended drop spring plates; in this way you can drop a set amount and the toe will be corrected to factory specs, giving you better handling and less tyre wear.

A variety of other products are available to lower the rear of a Bay Window, including adjustable spring plates, which are good for fine-tuning the ride height and horseshoe plates which bolt between the spring plate and hub, giving a 3in drop. The only issue with horseshoe plates is that they increase the rear track width by around 10mm, which means fitting horseshoes with certain aftermarket wheels isn't possible. Horseshoe plates can also break, which is a real safety issue.

When lowering the rear of a Bay Window more than 4-5in, it will be necessary to notch the chassis for driveshaft and/or swing arm clearance, depending on what method you have employed for the rear suspension modifications. If you are using horseshoe plates you can get away with a small notch for the driveshaft, but using other methods will necessitate a larger C-notch. There are now a few companies selling laser cut and welded frame notch kits, which make the job easier but do be aware that once done, it will be difficult to return to stock.

Raising a Bay Window

Similar to the Split Bus, there are raised spindles available for the Bay – companies like Old Speed in California, and Wagenswest can supply welded spindles. You can also use adjusters in the front beam, but if you raise the suspension more than an inch or two with adjusters, the flat torsion leaves in the front beam will be working in the wrong plane: this means very little – if any – springing. In extreme cases, you

Although my '72 Single Cab appears to have raised suspension in these pictures, the raise is purely as a result of the 27x8.5x14in Kumho Road Venture MT tyres. (Author's collection)

could use drop brackets welded to the beam – these enable the beam to be dropped lower – this will increase height, but not ground clearance.

When it comes to the rear of a Bay, either the suspension can be raised on the splines, or you could use bolt-on drop plates. When raising a Bay, similar to an IRS Beetle, you'll need to change to CV joints with a larger degree of travel – see the info in the IRS Beetle section above for CV advice.

Type 3 – Fastback, Squareback, Notchback, T34 Karmann Ghia

For the first time in the history of Volkswagen production, the Type 3 range had completely re-designed front suspension, utilising solid torsion bars, rather than leaves, which crossed over inside the front axle beam. This meant that Type 3 models were equipped with superior ride quality and handling.

While the accepted method for lowering and narrowing the front end of a Type 3 nowadays seems to be fitting a narrowed Type 1 beam assembly, this is actually a backwards move in terms of both ride quality and handling. The Type 1 beam conversions mainly came about because of

the need (or desire) to narrow the front suspension, and the realisation that it is very difficult to narrow the original Type 3 front beam because the solid torsion bars cross over and are splined at the outer ends.

Lower front (original beam)

To lower the Type 3 models with stock suspension, it's a simple matter of adjusting the torsion bars on the splines both in front and at the rear; a Type 3 lowered

Lowering a Type 3 on the standard suspension is a simple job, with only hand tools required. Gareth Bayliss-Smith's hardcore Patina Squareback looks great with Patina EMPI Sprintstar wheels. (Courtesy Gareth Bayliss-Smith)

Judith Wilding's original paint '62 Notchback lived its early life in the Austrian Tirol. After being driven daily, all year round, by Judith and partner, Vic, for a few years, it recently emerged from a metal restoration with some sympathetic paint blending by Ben Lewis at Evil Ben's. (Author's collection)

by this method, as long as carried out correctly, has always meant that lowered Type 3s retain good ride quality – as long as the original bump stops are removed. The main bugbear when lowering a Type 3 and retaining the original front beam, though, is that the lower frame horns, where the original beam attaches, hang down really low, causing clearance problems, even on moderately lowered cars.

There are things that can be done to increase ground clearance here: Ben Lewis (of Evil Ben's in Cornwall, UK) came up with a modification to

The Type 3 front beam is much more complicated than a Type 1 or Type 2 beam: the solid torsion bars cross over inside the beam, making narrowing it very hard. (Courtesy Gareth Bayliss-Smith)

the beam mounting area, making the frame head of cars less likely to hit the ground. When it comes to narrowing the front suspension, Old Speed in Paramount, California, have designed and built narrowed Type 3 front trailing arms and drop spindles, which are jig built and welded to a very high standard. These will narrow the front track width by around 1in per side, whilst keeping the original front suspension setup.

Type 1 conversion beams

Of course, if you want to go really low, then Type 1 conversion beams are available from a variety of suppliers, allowing you to fit either a link pin or ball joint Type 1 beam, complete with drop spindles, to the front of your Type 3. When fitting a Type 1 beam, it is necessary to remove the lower frame head horns from the front of the floorpan if you want to increase ground clearance, but doing this makes it very hard to put a car back to stock in future.

Rear suspension

Lowering the rear of a Type 3 is very similar to lowering the rear of a Bug; Type 3s were swing axle up to 1968, then IRS from 1969 onwards. Type 3s can be lowered by adjusting the spring plates on the splines, but this will affect toe in, so, if lowering more than a couple of inches, it's best to fit extended drop spring plates to the rear, doing so will give better handling and less tyre wear.

Built by Si and Jess Medlicott a few years ago, this Type 1 beam converted Nutria Brown Notchback now belongs to Dave Hall. (Author's collection)

Mini C-notches are often necessary when running flipped drop spindles; the modified spindle means that the steering arm sits higher up in relation to the trailing arms. (Author's collection)

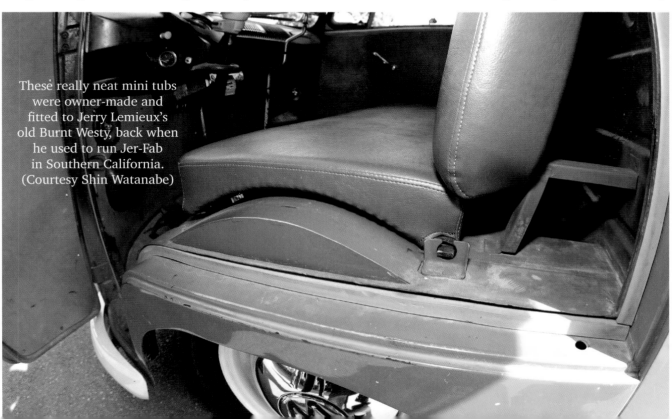

These really neat mini tubs were owner-made and fitted to Jerry Lemieux's old Burnt Westy, back when he used to run Jer-Fab in Southern California. (Courtesy Shin Watanabe)

Jason Reich's '58 Beetle had a mild lowering job but looked really good on its original EMPI Sprintstar wheels.
(Courtesy Jason Reich/Aircooled Vintage Works)

Chassis notches and wheel tubs

When you're lowering a Bus a lot, you'll eventually run into problems with even the smallest of tyres hitting underneath the wheelarches – raised tubs are the only solution if you're wanting to go this low. Various companies, such as Trailer Queen Restorations in the UK, offer pre-fabricated tubs that you can weld in. Drilling out the spot welds of the original tubs and keeping the original metal in case you, or the next owner, want to put the Bus back to stock is a wise option.

When it comes to chassis notches, these are often necessary for tie rod clearance on the front of a Bay or Split Bus, or for driveshaft and swing arm clearance on the back of a Bay Window – large C-notch tubs are available for Bays – these are based on the drawings that Franz Muhr from KCW put out on the internet when he made some many years ago. Bear in mind when making any chassis mods, that the thickness of the chassis rails really does count, especially if your Bus was ever in an accident.

Summary

This guide to carrying out suspension modifications to your Volkswagen isn't meant to be a step-by-step how-to, but is intended to explain what is available parts-wise, and to impart a few tips learned from years of lowering and raising air-cooled VWs. Please continue to be aware of safety when it comes to carrying out suspension and brake modifications, and realise that the lower you go, the more modifications to every moving part will be necessary in order for everything to function correctly.

Ultimately, what you do to your car is up to you, but do bear in mind the rarity of good cars now, and potential values when it comes to making modifications that will be either difficult or, in some cases, impossible to return to stock in the future. There are some people who think that heavy suspension modifications and hacks are like this generation's 1970s' cut rear wheelarches; lots of these modified cars will eventually be devalued because they can't be restored as easily.

CHAPTER SEVEN
Interiors & trim

How to achieve the right look for your car

When it comes to the interiors of Patina cars, it really is a case of anything goes; some choose to sympathetically restore the interior of a car to give it the survivor look, whereas others opt to leave as-is, or go for the fully restored interior look to contrast with the Patina paint outside. As with the many distinctly different paint looks, the interior of the cars can be dictated by what you purchase to begin with. This chapter explores the different looks involved, and shows the reader how to recreate them.

Way back when people began to modify VWs, often some pretty wild modifications were carried out to VW interiors. When the late '60s came along it was all about diamond stitched or Fat Biscuit upholstery, which gave way in the 1970s to aftermarket seats being fitted, as well as buttoned velours and shag-pile carpets. The '80s became more about outside graphics carried through to the interior, and an explosion of surf style fabric, which made for some pretty eye-watering interiors.

Around 1992, with renewed interest in traditional and 'Old School' Cal Looks, brought about by Keith Seume's book *California Look VW*, along with an interest in Resto Cal – cars with full original chrome trim and original interiors – full custom interiors began to take more of a back seat, and original style, or semi-original, with maybe some tweed inserts in the seats, began to gain – or regain – popularity.

Nowadays, when it comes to Patina VWs, the vast majority of owners favour either keeping the interior 100 per cent original, replacing the interior with a new interior kit from a company like TMI or Sewfine – companies that manufacture upholstery in the original VW OEM style – or a combination of the two. Although seat covers and door panel kits are still very popular – TMI is usually the manufacturer of choice for fairly correct styled interior kits and carpets – people are beginning to realise that the original VW upholstery, if still in serviceable or repairable condition, is actually a better bet than a new kit. There are various small differences in even the best new kit and original VW upholstery, be it thickness and durability of the vinyl, the cushioning in the door panels, or other small details that mean a lot to people who know what a correct interior should look like. It's for this reason, and the fact that getting new seat covers to fit without visible wrinkles is actually pretty difficult to achieve, people are realising that it's often much better to pay an upholsterer to save original seats, for example, than to discard them in favour of new.

Of course, there are still those who choose full-custom interiors, or to forge their own path when it comes to personalising the interior. Mexican blankets have always been popular in the American car scenes, and this has moved over to the VW scene. Where, once upon a time, a Mexican blanket was regarded as something cheap that you could cover up your shoddy upholstery with, some people now choose to have a car professionally upholstered using Mexican blankets.

Carpets and headliners are another area where some choose to use different style products to what was originally fitted – Volkswagen always used rubber mats for the floorboards of cars and Buses, but many owners now choose to carpet a car throughout, or to delete the headliner clips to run a smaller standard model type headliner and paint the surrounding metal. This chapter follows more of a gallery format – showing examples of cars with different styled interiors, so you can figure out what works for you and your car.

If you want to restore the interior of your car so it looks like it did when it left the factory, then there are examples of this, and tips on how to achieve it. Companies like West Coast Classics Restoration in Fullerton, California, have made a business out of reproducing some of the most correct VW interiors on the planet. Other companies, like Wolfsburg West in the USA, and Newton Commercial and Madmatz in the UK, produce accurately styled square weave carpets and original style rubber floor mats for those who want everything to be 100 per cent correct, or cheaper narrow weave carpets for those on a tighter budget. Even later model carpets are now catered for: the Perlon style carpet is available from Newton Commercial.

There really are no defined rules when it comes to building the interior for your car. Over the years, many fully restored cars have had the original interior paint left, as a testament to the originality of a car – many of these cars, it was felt, were let down by tired exterior paint, or the bodywork was heavily rusted to the point where it was felt that an exterior repaint was the only viable option. Maybe the outcome of the decision to repaint some of these cars would be different now, but many people still want to restore cars to look like new – this will never change.

As much as the VW industry tries to keep up with supplying new products – from body panels to new rubber and trim parts, the limitation will always be colour options. Volkswagen, especially in the 1960s, produced such a wide variety of complementary interior and exterior options, that it would be impossible to reproduce all of the original colours of rubber mats, running board mats or wing/fender beading. Contrary to popular belief, Volkswagen didn't often fit black wing/fender beading – it was usually body-coloured – and running board mats were rarely black throughout the '60s.

If you're looking to figure out what trim and colour options your car would have had originally, or what colour the steering wheel, gearlever or seat frames were, then you could do worse than to head over to the technical section of thesamba.com where you'll be able to see these options for all model years. Certain coloured running board mats are being reproduced by the likes of Wolfsburg West in California, but the range is limited to the more popular colours.

If your car colour falls outside of this, then a search

of thesamba.com classifieds or a visit to the website of a German collector, could net you the parts that you need – I once found a set of NOS (New Old Stock) Zenith Blue running board mats from the owner of www.kaefervwrostfrei.de who collects original running board mats and also manufactures great quality stainless steel running boards. If you have no success there, or can't afford the prices (I paid €400 for the last pair of Zenith Blue mats back in 2013) then you can dye black mats with a specialist vinyl or rubber paint. There's nothing that makes a car look better or more correct than the correct running board mats and wing/fender beading.

When it comes to interior rubber mats and parts, generally you'll have to put up with either finding good original parts or choosing from one or two stock colours, such as grey or black floormats. Again, parts such as floormats or parts like Type 3 dash pads can be dyed with colour matched specialist paint, if you really want a 100 per cent correct interior restoration. When it comes down to it, it's really great that many companies now reproduce countless VW parts that may be hard or even impossible to find, but there really is no substitute to original VW quality, be it a NOS or a good used part.

Take a look at the attached pictures in this chapter and the detailed captions; whatever the style of interior or exterior trim you decide on, there are tips here to help you achieve it. There are also mentions, where appropriate, of original style interior accessories, which can help give your interior more style points or add slightly to the creature comforts of spending many a mile behind the wheel of a vintage VW.

Opposite: The red rubber mats and carpets on this car are original and impossible to replace; luckily the interior on this car is in incredible condition. (Courtesy Gareth Cornell)

Gareth Cornell's rare '66 Saxomat semi automatic Beetle was discovered parked in a garage in Sussex, England with very low mileage. It's one of the rare Pigalle cars, which features a lot more red interior parts than regular red interior cars. (Courtesy Gareth Cornell)

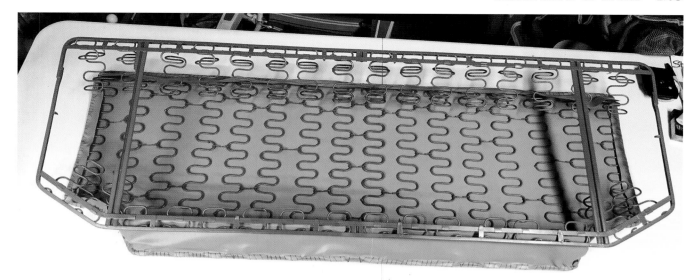

Above and opposite: Seth Wrobel chose to fit a 100 per cent new interior to his Turkis Beetle; the seat covers and door panels are from TMI and are Como Green/Phosphor – actually a colour combination on Turkis/Blue White Buses. The upholstery really suits the car. (Courtesy Seth Wrobel)

Coco mats were popular in the USA back when these cars were new; Austin chose to fit them in his car and they work well with the overall theme. (Courtesy Austin Working)

Diego Vazquez's clearcoated car has a slightly different take on an original interior, with upholstery modelled on early Karmann Ghia upholstery – it works well. (Courtesy David – BaitMedia)

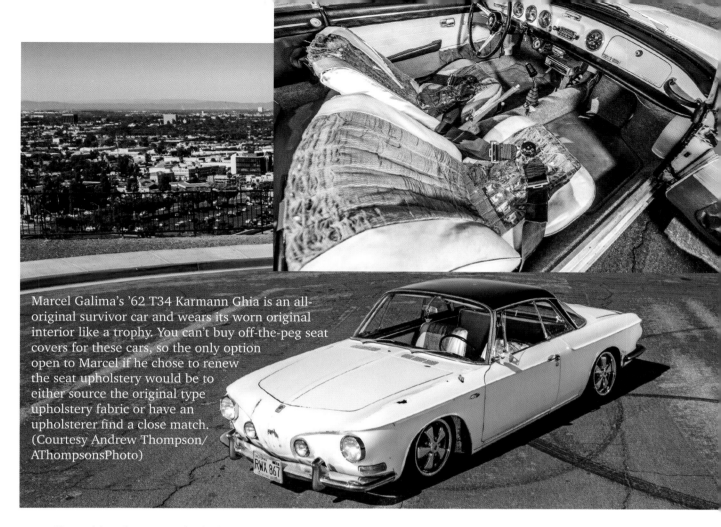

Marcel Galima's '62 T34 Karmann Ghia is an all-original survivor car and wears its worn original interior like a trophy. You can't buy off-the-peg seat covers for these cars, so the only option open to Marcel if he chose to renew the seat upholstery would be to either source the original type upholstery fabric or have an upholsterer find a close match. (Courtesy Andrew Thompson/ AThompsonsPhoto)

Bill Sembler chose to refresh the interior on his Beryl Green Bug with TMI interior panels; they are a great reproduction of the original style panels, although some die-hard purists will tell you that they are slightly too cushioned when compared to original. (Courtesy Bill Sembler)

Austin Working decided to backdate the interior of his awesome '68 Bug with smooth vinyl seat covers; the interior on this car had been toasted by the sun, so Austin decided to do the interior to show quality. Note the early style three-spoke steering wheel. (Courtesy Austin Working)

Johnny Montana chose a different route for his ongoing '62 Gulf Blue Bug; car guys have been fitting Mexican blankets to cover up old upholstery for years, but Johnny went one further and had some custom seat covers made up using Mexican blankets and a contrasting fabric. These will be fitted with the original grey/white door panels. (Courtesy Johnny Montana)

Craig Yelley tends to work with the original interior on the Buses he builds, and tries to save as much originality as possible – on this Bus he fitted new TMI seat covers, but cleaned up the original door panels, mats and headliner. (Courtesy Craig Yelley)

The main thing that attracted the owner of this '68 Beetle was the original blue running board mats and original blue wing/fender beading in the pictures he saw online; so few cars still have the original running boards fitted and even fewer have never had the wings removed. It proved to be a great indicator of condition. He drove 1600 miles to collect the car on a trailer in one weekend, without even having seen pictures of the underside of the car. It turned out to be a rust-free original survivor. (Author's collection)

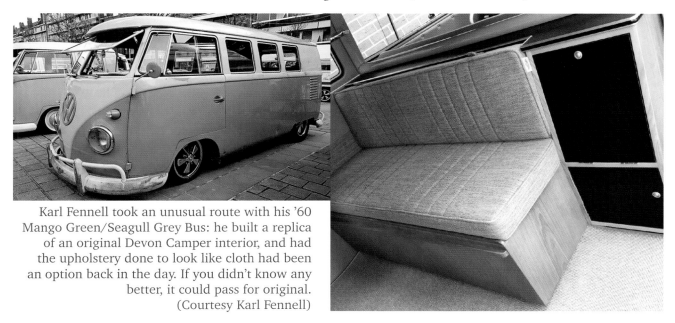

Karl Fennell took an unusual route with his '60 Mango Green/Seagull Grey Bus: he built a replica of an original Devon Camper interior, and had the upholstery done to look like cloth had been an option back in the day. If you didn't know any better, it could pass for original. (Courtesy Karl Fennell)

Billy Davila has a certain ethos when it comes to his insane Patina Turkis/Blue White 23-window deluxe Bus. He lives with what is there, unless a better original or NOS (New Old Stock) part comes along. Original parts, whilst hard to find, are still out there; Billy knows he'll never sell the Bus, so there's no urgency in the interior preservation/restoration. (Courtesy Andrew Thompson/AThompsonsPhoto)

Seth Wrobel and Nate Jones' cars have had the original style coloured running board mats replaced, and they look all the better for it. You can check on thesamba.com if your car colour would have had them fitted – they were fitted from 1961 until 1970. (Courtesy Seth Wrobel/Nate Jones)

Some NOS coloured running board mats I sourced recently for my '68 Beetle and the *Salvage Hunters* TV car. (Author's collection)

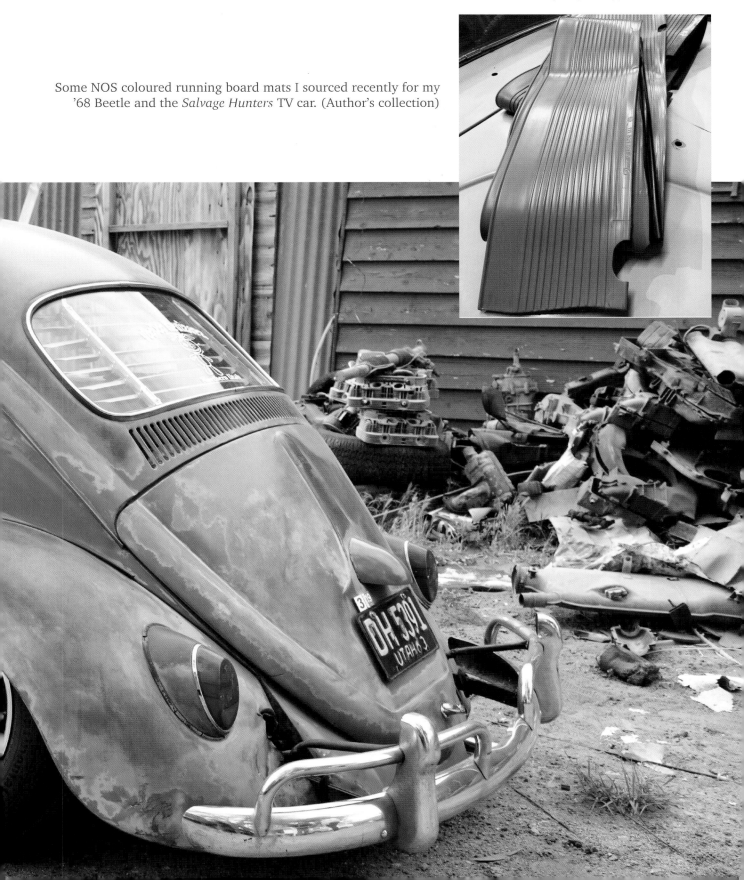

Randy and Alicia Slack's Convertible 'Burdie' is a true survivor; the interior was redone at some point over the years, but it suits the car really well and has a great Patina to it. To replace this interior with new would be crime. (Courtesy Andrew Thompson/ AThompsonsPhoto)

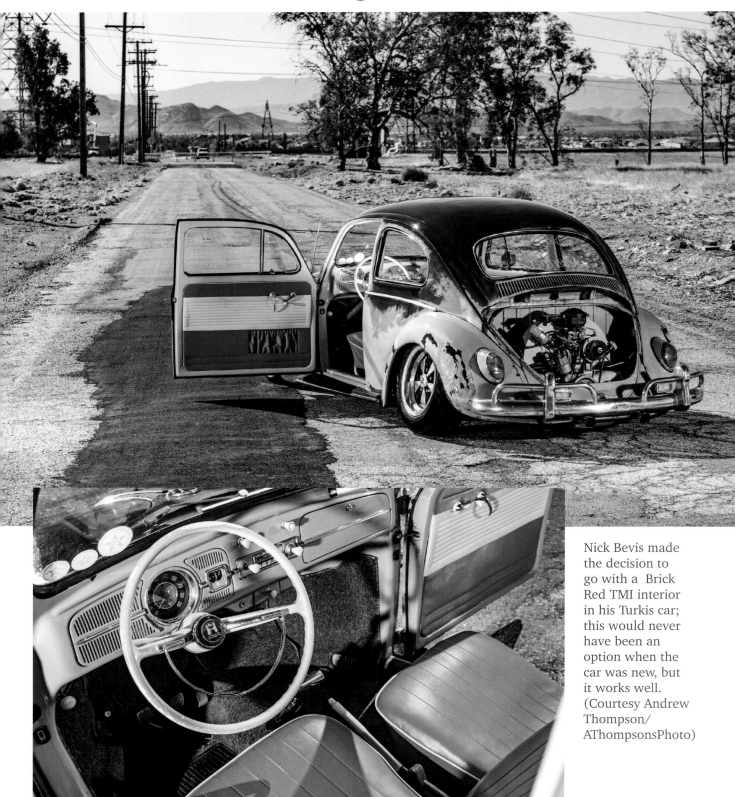

Nick Bevis made the decision to go with a Brick Red TMI interior in his Turkis car; this would never have been an option when the car was new, but it works well. (Courtesy Andrew Thompson/AThompsonsPhoto)

CHAPTER EIGHT
Finishing the look

As with any car, a successful Patina VW build takes into account many different elements that all need to work well together in order to end up with a car that looks right. In this chapter, we look at some of the cars which get the look right, and show the reader which elements – wheels, suspension, accessories – were used in order to create the finished look. We also look at the process and techniques involved in making new accessories appear old so that they work better with the overall look. This chapter also covers original company logos, and how they can be retouched or sympathetically restored.

It takes a lot of individual elements to make any project car build, and quite often it can be the small details that make a car look amazing … or not. You might absolutely nail the Patina matching on the paintwork and do a great and sympathetic job of restoring the original interior, but you may ruin it with your choice of wheels and tyres or stance. You might decide at the last minute to fit a few new accessories, which don't really go with all of the original Patina parts of the car. Like I said, building a car involves lots of small elements, but get one wrong and sometimes a car will just look wrong.

In this, the final chapter, we'll showcase a few different cars and comment on the finer points that make them work; it could be something as simple as the wheel and tyre choice on a car that makes it extra special, or it could be that all of the accessories used just simply work with the rest of the Patina. When it comes down to it, to build a car like this successfully, you need to be a particular type of person. Some would call it particular, others would call it being anal. Whatever you want to call it, it's the type of illness that takes over your whole being – the quest for originality and to ace the finer details of your build.

Randy and Alicia Slack's '57 Karmann Kab has it going on, with the right choice of rare accessories and the right tyres – you can't beat whitewall crossplies on a stock height '50s VW – especially a Kab. (Courtesy Andrew Thompson/AThompsonsPhoto)

For Patina guys and girls, it's not about buying new parts off the shelf, it's about finding original parts that suit the look of the car, such as this Patina Deluxe horn push; it takes pride of place on the steering wheel of Billy Davila's Deluxe Bus. (Courtesy Andrew Thompson/AThompsonsPhoto)

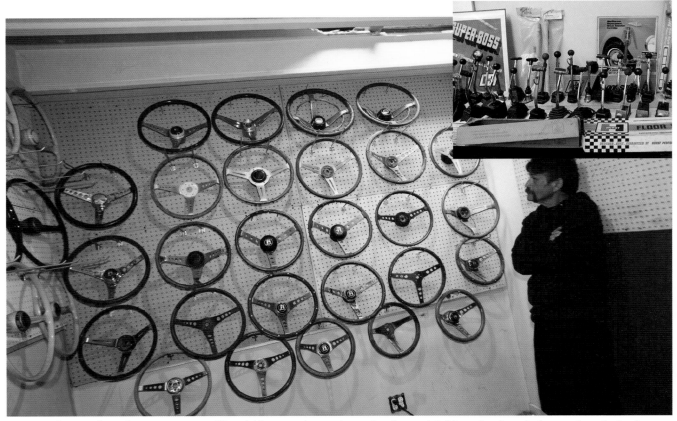

Original period performance parts like shifters and steering wheels are highly prized and change hands for large sums of money. (Bottom: Courtesy Julien-David Collombet/*Super VW Magazine*. Right/inset: Courtesy Chadd Magee)

I spent a long time trying to make the Mobil Pegasus on my '67 Beetle look like an original one, staining it with tea, then adding satin lacquer. (Author's collection)

Martin Feast's '70 Deluxe shows the lengths some people go to in order to source period correct parts. Martin trades in original water slide travel decals, but also has a thing for using original, period-correct textiles, such as the curtains in the picture. (Courtesy Martin Feast)

With my help, Ed Massink found an original Volkswagen of America late Bug roofrack with Patina: a new roofrack on the Patina car just didn't look right. (Courtesy Ed Massink)

Original Westfalia roofracks, like that on Billy Davila's Bus, are highly prized and very valuable; you can buy perfect reproduction racks, but an original one will always be more sought after. (Courtesy Andrew Thompson/AThompsonsPhoto)

Johnny Montana chose to leave the Patina on his Swedish roofrack, just adding new slats and some wax. (Courtesy Johnny Montana)

I removed the aged hardwood slats from my 1950s Swedish roofrack and numbered them so they could reinstalled correctly once it had been repainted: the original paint was in too bad a condition to keep. (Author's collection)

Johnny Montana repurposed a set of 1950s Beetle ski racks to carry one of his vintage longboard skateboards, which he made out of vintage water skis. (Courtesy Johnny Montana)

Original US licence plate frames and license toppers are a nice finishing touch to a car that spent its life stateside. (Author's collection)

Restoring the original number plates on my '67 Beetle; the plate backing plates were in poor condition, but the digits have a nice Patina. (Author's collection)

Original paint nose badges for Split Buses now change hands for large sums of money, and it's easy to see why; the sun baked the badge on my '66 over five decades. (Author's collection)

A chance bargain swapmeet find, these accessory rear light lenses with round reflectors will add that small extra detail to Johnny Montana's '62. (Courtesy Johnny Montana)

My
original paint
'67 Kombi sporting
original Swedish
headlamp gravel guards
and original HWE roofrack – the
finer details really finish off a build.
(Author's collection)

Cody Goss has a thing for buying and carrying out a preservation style restoration on original paint wheels; there's a ready market, especially as wheels tend to go missing or lead a harder life than the rest of a car's paintwork.
(Courtesy Cody Goss)

Original paint commercial hubcaps too are very sought after nowadays – Everett Barnes' '61 Double Cab sports a set, but the wheels and hubcaps are freshly painted; many people like the fresh look of repainted bumpers and wheels on a Patina Bus. (Courtesy Everett Barnes/thesamba.com)

Original EMPI wheels, such as these early 5x205 Sprintstars in Danny Zepeda's collection are worth their weight in gold. (Courtesy Julien-David Collombet/*Super VW Magazine*)

Original used or NOS accessory wheel embellishers, such as these fitted to my '66 Beetle, are an easy and fairly cheap way of giving a car a different look. (Author's collection)

Andre Burchard has a thing for Buses with original logos. After paying a sign painter to re-touch the logos on his first logo Bus, he then decided that he could do it himself. Andre has to be the world's most prolific logoed Bus builder. (Courtesy Andre Burchard)

A couple of the original logo Buses that Andre has carried out a preservation type restoration on; often the logos on these Buses were barely visible when the vehicles were discovered, having just an outline left. (Courtesy Andre Burchard)

Original logos are seen as cool in the VW scene, as are rare wheels; the Bob Saunders Bus has both, with amazing original logos and rare Brahim Racing wheels. (Author's collection)

Is this the future of the Patina VW? Both Christopher Dozier's silver car 'Melanoma' and Eddie Davis' Green 1980 three-door Rabbit have great Patina and the owners wouldn't have it any other way. It's taking a long time for the water-cooled VW scene to embrace Patina, but these guys are among the pioneers. (Courtesy Christopher Dozier/Eddie Davis)

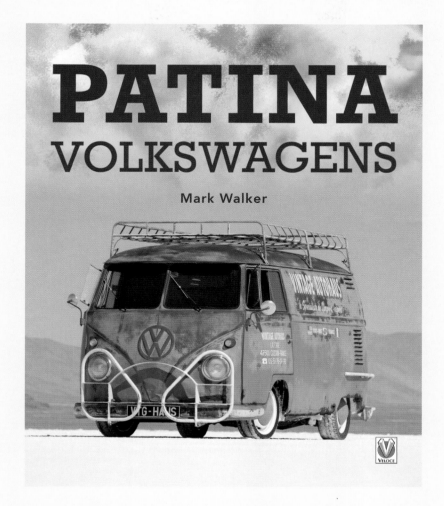

Patina Volkswagens is the first book to look at how and why Volkswagens with original paint and patina have become so popular. The book explores the many different facets of this trending hobby, from the cars themselves, to the owners and the global scene surrounding them.

ISBN: 978-1-787113-15-2
Hardback • 25x20.7cm • 160 pages
• 318 colour and b&w pictures

More great Volkswagen books from Veloce ...

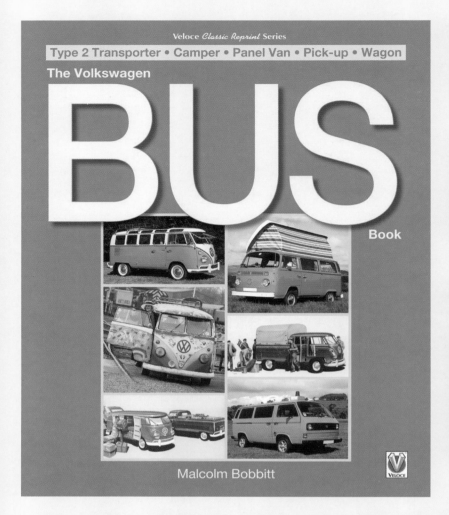

Veloce Classic Reprint Series

Type 2 Transporter • Camper • Panel Van • Pick-up • Wagon

The Volkswagen

BUS

Book

Malcolm Bobbitt

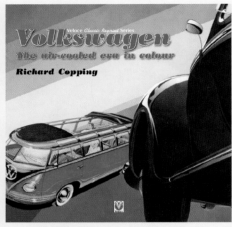

ISBN: 978-1-787111-21-9

ISBN: 978-1-787113-01-5

Researched in incredible detail, this book explores the story of the timeless VW Bus, from early origins through to the present day. This entirely new edition includes details of many of the different camper conversions, and examines the social history and the T2's evolution. Including full specifications, production figures and buying advice, this is a must for any VW enthusiast.

ISBN: 978-1-845849-95-5
Paperback • 25x20.7cm • 208 pages
• 258 colour and b&w pictures

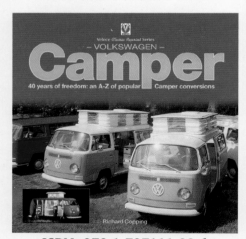

ISBN: 978-1-787111-22-6

For more information and price details, visit our website at www.veloce.co.uk
email: info@veloce.co.uk • Tel: +44(0)1305 260068

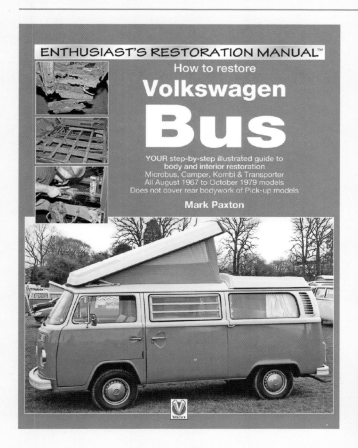

The only book currently available that comprehensively deals with the realities of restoring a VW Bay Window Bus. With over 1500 mainly colour photos, it guides the reader clearly through body and chassis repairs, paintwork, interior re-trimming and most common mechanical problems. The skills, techniques and even the tools needed to complete these tasks are explained in jargon free language, to ensure that even those enthusiasts with no previous restoration experience will feel confident in sorting out their Bus. An indispensable and unique guide for lovers of these fast appreciating classics.

ISBN: 978-1-845840-93-8
Paperback • 27x20.7cm • 272 pages
• 1110 colour and b&w pictures

Written by an enthusiast the How to Restore Volkswagen Beetle Enthusiasts Restoration Manual is the only up-to-date book dealing with a complete Beetle restoration – from basic skills required, to dealing with professional restorers. The perfect book, whether you have no technical knowledge, or are an old hand at restoring!

ISBN: 978-1-845849-46-7
Paperback • 27x20.7cm • 224 pages
• 700 colour pictures

For more information and price details, visit our website at www.veloce.co.uk
email: info@veloce.co.uk • Tel: +44(0)1305 260068

Volkswagen modification guides from Veloce ...

How to get the best handling and braking from your Volkswagen Beetle. Covers front and rear suspension, chassis integrity, suspension geometry, ride height, camber, castor, kpi, springs, shock absorbers, testing and adjustment.

ISBN: 978-1-903706-99-2
Paperback • 25x20.7cm • 128 pages

The complete practical guide to modifying classic to modern VW Bus (Transporter) T1 to T5 suspension, brakes and chassis for maximum performance. Contains essential information on using aftermarket parts and interchangeable parts from other production vehicles to achieve great handling (and a lower stance if required). This edition includes many new photographs and archive pictures plus an additional 16 pages of information.

ISBN: 978-1-845842-62-8
Paperback • 25x20.7cm • 144 pages
• 460 pictures

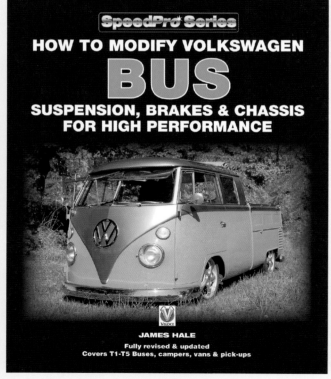

For more information and price details, visit our website at www.veloce.co.uk
email: info@veloce.co.uk • Tel: +44(0)1305 260068

Index